home*girl*

home girl

The Single Woman's Guide to Buying Real Estate in Canada

Brenda Bouw

BICENTENNIAL
1807
WILEY
2007
BICENTENNIAL

John Wiley & Sons Canada, Ltd.

National Library of Canada Cataloguing in Publication Data

Bouw, Brenda
   Home girl : the single woman's guide to buying real estate in Canada /
Brenda Bouw.

Includes index.
ISBN: 978-0-470-83924-9

   1. House buying—Canada. 2. Single women—Housing—Canada. 3. Real estate investment—Canada. I. Title.

HD1379.B68 2007   643'.12086520971   C2006-905920-9

The material in this publication is provided for information purposes only. Laws, regulations, and procedures are constantly changing, and the examples given are intended to be general guidelines only. This book is sold with the understanding that neither the author nor the publisher is engaged in rendering professional advice. It is strongly recommended that legal, accounting, tax, financial, insurance, and other advice or assistance be obtained before acting on any information contained in this book. If such advice or other assistance is required, the personal services of a competent professional should be sought.

Material used from Canada Mortgage and Housing Corporation (CMHC): *Home Maintenance Schedule, Before You Renovate, Your Guide to Renting a Home*, www.cmhc.ca, 2006. All Rights Reserved. Reproduced with the consent of CMHC. All other uses and reproductions of this material are expressly prohibited.

Production Credits
Cover and interior text design: Jason Vandenberg
Wiley Bicentennial Logo: Richard J. Pacifico
Printer: Printcrafters

John Wiley & Sons Canada, Ltd.
6045 Freemont Blvd.
Mississauga, Ontario
L5R 4J3

Printed in Canada

2 3 4 5 PC 11 10 09 08 07

Contents

Foreword

*H*ome Girl could really be called *Home Girl, Investment Girl, Taking Control Girl*. Women of all ages (both married and single) have become a powerful force in the real estate market. This remarkable book provides you with a step-by-step guide that will allow you to cut through the hype and misinformation that surrounds the real estate market. It will open doors for you, both literally and figuratively.

Imagine walking into your own home, a home you own yourself. No one to answer to, no one to have to ask permission of. You choose the colours, you choose the décor; you can put your own unique signature throughout. Your tastes change, you can change it on a whim… making it a place you are proud to call home.

In Canada today, this dream is more possible for single women than ever before, and this book is the key to achieving the dream.

The strategies and insights provided in this book are for you if:

- You're tired of paying rent and want to buy your first home—and want a step-by-step guide

- You're not quite sure if buying is better than renting and you want an honest answer

- You already own your own home but would like to buy an investment property in your neighbourhood

- You want to avoid mistakes others have made and want to make buying your home an enjoyable and stress-free experience

In other words, it will help you answer the critical question: **Are You Truly Ready to Jump into the Real Estate Market, or Not?**

Single women throughout Canada are taking charge of their financial futures by getting into the real estate market…but you'll soon find out it is not for everyone.

Home Girl is filled with shameless honesty. Brenda Bouw has held nothing back, revealing both the blemishes as well as the wonderful opportunities home ownership can provide the single woman. This is not a sugar-coated fantasyland book about real estate. This is one of the most balanced and honest looks at the real estate market you will ever find. It is critical that you have all the facts, and this book hands them to you.

You will hear, in their own words, women from across the country sharing mistakes they made (so you can avoid making them) as well as amazing stories of triumph. In this way, the book uncovers and deals directly with the key components you need to understand, delivering the information in an easy conversational tone. You'll hear secrets about:

- Financing options and the single woman
- Maintaining your property, whether you do it yourself or not
- Finding the exact right realtor; it is often not whom you think
- How to address safety and security issues *before* you buy
- How expensive of a property can you really afford?
- What to say and what *not* to say when negotiating your deal
- How to dramatically reduce the risk of buying your own home
- The tax-free financial freedom that owning your own home can provide you
- How to deal with having very little as a down payment or a low income
- And much more

You're provided with a checklist, action steps and, most importantly, the knowledge and confidence to move forward. What this book does is turn the complex act of purchasing a property into a step-by-step formula, and it does it all with flat-out honesty.

If you are even remotely curious about the unique problems (and the solutions) that single women have when buying real estate in today's market, this book is a must read. It may just be time for you to join the dramatically growing community of single women homeowners and investors.

Live your dreams, have the freedom to make your home your own. There is no stopping you now.

Don R. Campbell
Best-selling author of *Real Estate Investing in Canada*
www.reincanada.com

Acknowledgements

This book would not have been possible without the friendship and support of author/journalist Paul Brent, and his wife Mary Donohue. To them, I am forever thankful.

I would also like to credit my editor, Don Loney, who came to me with the great idea about a book geared toward single woman buying real estate. He then left the approach of the book to me, based on my personal experience. Nicole Langlois, another single woman homebuyer, also deserves kudos for her sharp edit of the manuscript. Author/journalist Tony Martin was also a huge help in setting me up for the challenge of writing my first book.

Thanks to the many real estate and financial professionals quoted in the book, whose information and advice will be invaluable to all single women buying, or considering buying real estate. A special thanks to my friend and real estate agent Darren Josephs, who answered a lot of my questions and, in doing so, helped strengthen the information and advice you read here. Darren, along with realtor Doug Heldman, real estate author Don Campbell, friends Natalie Armstrong and Allison Grace, and sisters Kristine and Karen Bouw, all proofread parts of the manuscript, offering valuable feedback. Thanks also to the rest of my family members for their support.

Finally, a huge thanks to all of the brave and smart single women homebuyers (and those considering it) who shared their personal stories told in this book. Without them, this adventure would not have been nearly as fun.

Introduction

It was the night before she was to put in an offer on a downtown Toronto loft that my friend Jennifer—a tough-as-nails event producer—turned to me, a little weepy. "I want this place. I love it. I just thought it would be something I'd do with another person—a husband, you know."

They were the last tears she would shed over that purchase, which proved to be one of the best investment decisions of Jennifer's life. That 715-square-foot space she bought in the summer of 2002 for $215,000, in one of Toronto's hottest neighbourhoods, is appreciating nicely. It is also now being put to very good use. A little more than a year after buying her condo, Jennifer found her Mr. Right. Soon after, she moved into his townhouse in the city's west end, followed months later by their dog, Sam. As for that loft space she owns, Jennifer uses it as office space, having left her full-time job at a major media company and starting her own event management business.

Looking back, Jennifer says buying that place was a personal achievement. Doing it on her own also gave her the confidence to make other major life decisions, such as starting her own company.

"It was just something I knew I needed to do on my own, regardless of who was with me or not with me," Jennifer says of the condo purchase. "It's serendipitous that it is now being used for office space."

Jennifer is part of an unstoppable trend in North America—single women buying real estate. No more waiting for Mr. Right.

Statistics show single Canadian women now make up a huge portion of the home-buying public. Royal LePage Real Estate Services released a survey in 2004 showing 51 percent of women were first-time homebuyers, compared to 49 percent of men. As well, of those who have never owned a home, 55 percent of women said they expected to buy their first home before 2008, compared to 45 percent of men.

"We have seen a marked change in the attitudes of women toward home ownership over the past several years," Royal LePage president and CEO Phil Soper said at the release of their homebuyers report. "Traditionally, marriage came before the mortgage, but goals have clearly changed. Women are using their purchasing power to invest in real estate and have little trepidation about doing it alone."

Since the report was released, the trend has grown stronger, says Dianne Usher, a vice-president with Royal LePage. She says single women are not only more independent today, but many are also earning higher incomes. "What I'm seeing is real estate being considered increasingly, not just as the cornerstone of one's portfolio, but as a really good place to put money, whether for investment purposes or for a roof over your head." Dianne says she has been surprised by the number of young women buying property early in their careers. "Instead of going into rental accommodation they are out buying condos on their own."

Royal LePage representatives say they were surprised by the study's findings showing 30 percent of women said they would be "very likely" to forgo a wedding reception to put a larger down payment on their first home, compared to 15 percent of men.

The surprise here isn't that fewer men would skip the reception; after all, it's traditional for the bride's family to pay for most or all of the wedding. Instead, it's that fewer women want the white wedding, and would rather have a reliable roof over their head.

Jennifer, whom you met earlier, made a wedding pact with her father just before she bought her loft. Instead of paying for a wedding someday, as they did for her big sister, she suggested putting that money towards a down payment for property.

His reaction?

"He loved the idea! He always thought the idea of spending money on a wedding was ridiculous," Jennifer says. She matched the amount of his gift through her own savings and as a result was able to lower her mortgage payments to a comfortable level. "All of a sudden I was in the right place at the right time, where I could make this happen," she recalls.

The spinoff of the hike in female home ownership is obvious in the new female-friendly Home Depots and the growing list of home improvement shows hosted, and watched, by women. Even Carrie Bradshaw, the ditsy diva with the Manolo Blahnik fetish from HBO's *Sex and the City*, bought property.

Count me in on that trend. In fact, I may have slightly skewed the Canadian statistics on female home ownership, having bought and sold three properties while I was between the ages of 30 and 34. Every place was meant to be a longer-term investment, but life happens.

My first purchase was an old rowhouse in downtown Toronto. I did some minor renovations on my own, with the help of my friends, and sold it 10 months later for a profit. My next home was a detached, three-bedroom home on a quiet street in Hamilton, Ontario. The price was ridiculously cheap by Toronto standards, and apart from adding a new furnace and central air conditioner, I didn't have to fix a thing when I moved in.

While living in Hamilton, I bought a retrofitted loft in a gritty east-side Toronto neighbourhood from a builder's floor plan. It was meant as an investment property, but I was lured back to Toronto for a job, and sold my Hamilton home just in time to move in to the loft. But after two years of downtown loft living—and one too many arguments with the local crack addicts—I sold the space. I went back to renting, deciding to wait until I am ready to own a home again.

Looking back, I have my horror stories of home ownership: endless negotiations, derelict neighbours, cockroaches and leaky roofs. I made some mistakes along the way, but I also made some money. These experiences, along with the stories shared by dozens of other single women in this book, will help women of any age or circumstance who are considering going it alone in home ownership.

This book will take you through the home-buying process as seen through the eyes of single women across Canada. Women of all ages and circumstances (single, widowed and divorced) tell you about their good and bad experiences of buying (and selling) homes. You will get their advice on what they did right (and wrong) and what they wish someone had told them the first time they bought property. Each chapter will end with a checklist of things to do, and a list of common mistakes to avoid.

This book will also help you discover if you are ready for home ownership—which, of course, not all single women are. Buying a home on your own is a huge achievement, but it is not for everyone. Reading through these pages will help you determine if you are ready and able to make the commitment. If not, hold on to this book for when your time comes.

Remember as you read, consider and plan that buying and selling property is not unlike dating—the more you do it, the more you learn what you want. My goal is to help women buy right the first time.

1

Are You

Ready?

_A_ngela Nolan was 29 years old when she announced to friends and colleagues she was buying a house—by herself.

"People looked at me like I had three heads. It was kind of like the look my guidance counsellor gave me in high school when I said I wanted to be an air traffic controller. He said 'You mean an airline stewardess?'" recalls Angela, now in her forties—and a real estate agent, not an air traffic controller. "People didn't take me seriously about the house at the time. My co-workers didn't think it was viable."

She did it anyway. In 1991 she bought a five-bedroom home on a quiet street in west Hamilton, Ontario, for the asking price of $140,000. Angela stayed in that home for 10 years. To help with the mortgage, she rented a room to a Japanese exchange student. A few years later she got married, and her husband moved in. The couple had two sons, both of whom were raised in that house until the ages of six and seven. Angela and her husband sold the house in 2001 for $160,000 and bought a bigger place, for $189,000, to better fit their growing boys.

Looking back, Angela says buying that first home on her own put her a step ahead when it came time to raise a family. Not only did she build equity, but because she purchased the home on her own she knew the monthly payments could be managed on one income.

"It meant I was able to stay home with my kids because I had that house. When I considered going back to work, I said the only way I would go back was if we put every penny I made back into the mortgage." Now that she's a real estate agent in Hamilton, Angela says her decision to buy solo was a smart investment, both personally and financially. "Having a house makes you a more attractive single girl. The alternative is that you sit back and say, 'Oh, I'm just waiting for someone to help me and save me and take care of me.' I'm not the damsel-in-distress type."

Erica, a twenty-something journalism school graduate, believes waiting for a man before buying property is "as ridiculous as waiting for hell to freeze over." Erica bought a condo in downtown Toronto a few years after the death of her father, one of the 24 Canadian victims of the September 11, 2001, terrorist attacks. Rather than sue, Erica's family opted for the victims' compensation package. She could have invested the money in the markets, but instead chose to invest in a living space for herself.

"I am proud to come from a long line of independent women," says Erica. "And my mom always told me to be the man I want to marry." For Erica, that meant being independent and making smart financial decisions. She says she is now hooked on real estate. Her goal down the road is to buy more properties for investment purposes. "I know there's a lot to learn, but I've never been afraid of putting in the effort, especially when I consider how great the rewards are."

Christiane, a manager for a Toronto-based book publisher, bought a house at age 33, after 13 years of paying rent in downtown Toronto and realizing the white picket fence and 1950s "June Cleaver waiting-for-a-man lifestyle" was a thing of the past. "Too many women think that's what you have to do—find a boy, get engaged, blah, blah, blah. Ditch that idea. If you have a decent job, go for it," Christiane advises. "For me, there was always a good reason to put it off. But looking back at all the money I threw away in rent, I regret waiting so long to buy on my own. You're never too young to do it."

Buying Smart and Solo

Everyone has a story about buying and selling real estate. No two are the same. Even the strongest and smartest women out there have made mistakes along the way. Many have also made money. But before you go plunking your savings down on a house or condo, be sure you are ready.

It's a big step, and, yes, it can be scary. The best way to fight that fear is to get educated. It's true what they say: buying a home is one of the biggest emotional and financial decisions you will ever make. This includes first-time buyers and fifth-time buyers. Every time you buy you learn something about the process. I did, all three times.

I bought my first home at age 30. It was 2001. Interest rates were low and I had no plans to marry. I had heard of other single women taking the homeowner plunge and believed if they could do it, so could I. I started, as most do nowadays when looking for a home, by surfing mls.ca, the online Multiple Listing Service. It became my porn. I spent hours searching for properties in dozens of price ranges in a handful of neighbourhoods. Finally, I decided to actually go out and see some of those places in person.

I bought the first house I saw. My agent, Darren Josephs—now also a good friend—insisted I see other homes before making an offer. I was sure this strategy was a waste of time, but Darren insisted. I saw what I could get for more money, and what I could get if I paid less (I think it was advertised as a "handyman's special"—you know the kind). Darren was right. Seeing those others homes confirmed my decision; I was ready to buy.

Not everyone is ready to buy property—or, at least, not as ready as they might think.

For Natalie, a Toronto-based journalist, it took an episode of cold feet before she knew she was ready to buy her downtown condo. For about eight months she looked at dozens of places. Some were too big, others too small. None were quite right. One day she stumbled upon a condo that seemed to be the one—a two-storey unit in a low-rise building on the western edge of downtown, for about $160,000. She decided to make an offer and called her agent to set it up. But then, just before she was to make the offer, she backed out. "I panicked. I guess I just wasn't ready after all."

Natalie took the summer off from house hunting, and moved in with a roommate she nicknamed the "eternal bachelor." Naked hot tub parties (she didn't attend), the 42-inch TV forever tuned to such shows as *Blind Date* or *Jackass*, and a never-ending string of female overnight guests (he even once confessed to breaking the bed!). It was not at all like the camaraderie she had shared with her two previous male roommates before one moved in with his girlfriend and the other went off to pursue a music career. When the members of that happy home went their separate ways, Natalie was left to find a new living arrangement. But being a chaperone to the eternal bachelor was more than she bargained for. Natalie was ready to buy.

"I knew I had to get out of my current living situation and take the plunge. I was ready," Natalie says. She called her agent. Within a week, she saw a handful of condos and put in an offer on a two-bedroom condo on the lower floor of a high-rise. The price they were asking was low by Toronto standards—only $220,000—and definitely calculated to create a bidding war for the space. The cost was slightly above her price range, but Natalie figured she would risk taking on a roommate if necessary to help her pay the bills. She put in her offer, but lost to a higher bidder.

Slightly discouraged, but determined to find her own place, Natalie kept hunting. A week later, she saw a 700-square-foot, one-bedroom condo on the fourth floor of a building just steps from the city's eclectic Kensington Market neighbourhood.

"I remember walking in, standing by the sliding patio door, and I looked at my agent, he looked at me and we both smiled. He said, 'This is it, isn't it?' It was," she recalls of that November day in 2003. Not only was the place perfect for her, but she could afford the price tag of just over $200,000 without the risk of taking on a roommate. What's more, there was no bidding war. She moved in just before Christmas.

"In hindsight, I'm glad I got the cold feet before," Natalie says. "Everyone says, 'Oh, you will know when you find the right one.' They say that about relationships. I'm not sure about relationships, but it is true in the real estate department. If I had seen that place at the start—kind of like dating again, I would probably have wondered what else was out there. For me, it was good to 'try on' a few places first. Then I knew what I had."

So how do you know when the time is right for you? Checking your emotions is a good first step, but there are also some practical questions to ask yourself. The Canada Mortgage and Housing Corporation (CMHC) suggests that potential buyers ask themselves the following three questions:

1. Do you enjoy moving often?

2. Do you prefer using your savings for such things as vacations, retirement or starting your own business?

3. Do you enjoy not having to worry about regular maintenance and repairs?

If you answered yes to any of these questions, then maybe, just maybe, you aren't ready to buy a home. Remember that buying property means investing not just your hard-earned money, but a lot of time and energy. It also means making a commitment. Sure, you don't have to answer to the landlord and you can paint those walls any colour your heart desires, but there is a lot of financial stress when buying a home. First, you have a mortgage that you have to pay monthly. The consequences of missing a payment can wreak havoc with your credit rating. Second, you have to take care of the place—and that means when the basement floods, the plumbing needs repair and the roof leaks, you have to find the money and the right person to fix it. It's certainly not impossible. However, it can be stressful.

Karen, a twenty-something school teacher in Burford, Ontario, bought her first home at age 24, shortly after landing her first job. Making the mortgage was a struggle at first. However, Karen was proud to own her own home, instead of paying rent, especially so early in her career.

That said, she says the pressures of home ownership, especially as a single woman, can sometimes be overwhelming. "It's good equity. I cannot complain about that, but it can be very stressful. There are a lot of decisions to make. Between starting a career and having a house, it was nothing but decisions, decisions, decisions all the time for the first little while there. It's not that I had a problem making a decision, but it gets stressful and you often aren't sure if you are making the right one. Sometimes you want someone to say 'Do it this way' or 'Yes, you should call a plumber for that,' instead of always having to figure it out on your own. Sometimes you just need a break from decision-making."

Now that she's been a homeowner for a few years, Karen says she's not only better at making those choices, but says she's become more independent, and learned quite a bit along the way. "It's not for everyone," Karen says of single-woman home ownership, "but I think a lot of people don't realize they can actually do it."

Renting vs. Owning

Jennifer, whom you met in the introduction, started thinking seriously about buying while living on the first floor of a two-storey home in the beautiful Beach neighbourhood in east-end Toronto. Her landlord, who lived upstairs in the house, would sometimes knock on her door late at night, dressed in jeans and his white undershirt, to check in. Jennifer not only craved privacy but her own space. "I thought to myself, if this guy can own a home, so can I," she says.

Of course not all landlords are bad people, and if you are a bit of a rolling stone, or simply don't want the responsibility of owing property, renting might be best.

Take Brenda, a forty-something venture capitalist in Vancouver, who rents a beautiful apartment just blocks from the beach, on the main floor of a heritage home in the city's moneyed Point Grey neighbourhood. While she makes good money in her career, she cannot afford to buy a property in that area without seriously compromising the lifestyle she now enjoys.

"The number one reason I haven't bought is the change of lifestyle it would require," Brenda says. "I have witnessed so many single friends who, as soon as that purchase has been made, have no more spontaneous weekends. They are focussed on the house and that focus lasts a really long time. I think selfishly of how that has impacted my life. I have run out of people to have spontaneous trips with. They are not going out. The disposable income has dried up. It's a dramatic change for everyone."

Meanwhile, friends and colleagues have put pressure on her to join the homeowner club. "There are very few peers in my business who are still renting. Sometimes I feel like a social outcast."

Brenda sought the advice of a financial planner. "Am I crazy not to be buying?" she asked. "What should I be doing with my money?"

Her planner brought calm. "He said, 'You work too hard to feel like you cannot have the flexibility of trying to have a balanced life,'" Brenda recalls from the conversation. The financial planner advised her to ignore the peer pressure over buying property, and do what was best for her. What would make her happier: spending time and money on owning and maintaining a home, or on leisure activities such as travel?

"I think my life would be more stressful if I was tapped out with a mortgage," says Brenda. "It's not like I'm rolling in dough, but I have a reasonable income that allows me to accrue cash to do things like go to Africa. There is not a hope that I would have been able to do that as a homeowner."

Someday, Brenda says, she will buy a home, and she is setting aside money to make that purchase when she is ready.

Kim, a thirty-something who works in the Toronto media, rents in the city's plush High Park neighbourhood. She started renting on a month-by-month basis, but has been living in that apartment now for more than four years. She wants to buy property, but the high prices and commitment necessary to own have been obstacles so far.

"I started looking recreationally a few years ago. The idea then was that the market was going up and I'd be foolish not to get in right away. I did a lot of online cruising and went to a lot of open houses. I came back so depressed because I was looking at half-million-dollar crack houses," Kim recalls. "It was one of the most demotivating things I have ever done in my life."

For her, the pressure to buy is coming from her parents. "They want me to settle down; it would be an indicator for them that I've matured. I've also talked about having kids on my own. The precursor would be to have a stable living situation."

Kim admits a part of her may also be holding off for Mr. Right. "For the longest time I would have said that was not the case, but I think, yes, it would be really nice to buy with someone. The financial burden of sharing a house with someone would be significantly less— that is there. Also, it is harder for one person to have a house and have someone else move in as opposed to buying that house together."

Overall, Kim says buying a home is just too big a purchase for her to make decisively. "It's a lot of money. I am quick on most purchases and decisions in my life. On this one, I've been extraordinarily slow."

Her standards are also very high when it comes to the kind of home she wants to buy. "I want a place, ideally, that is beautiful. It has to have a yard, has to be in a safe neighbourhood and a friendly neighbourhood. I am actually picturing a white house, kind of like a cottage with a yard that is nicely fenced in. I want access to the city without living in the city." In other words, she wants the perfect house, which she knows sounds impractical. "I look for a house like I look for a man. Part of the process is that the perfect house doesn't exist—just like a man. Part of the process is to turn a house into Prince Charming. You grow together, you learn together. I think finding a house is the same. You have to grow with it, to make it your own."

Kim thinks she will eventually buy a home if she sets a deadline for herself. First, she has to be ready to pick a date.

- - - -

To compare the costs of renting versus buying, there are a number of calculators you can access through a quick Google search online. These are useful, but they don't take into consideration the lifestyle choices that are really behind the decision to buy a home (or not to buy).

Another thing to consider when deciding whether to rent or buy is, of course, housing prices. They have gone up considerably in recent years, especially in large cities such as Toronto, Ottawa, Vancouver, Winnipeg, Calgary and Edmonton. While housing prices have jumped, low mortgage rates have opened up the market to many people who might not have been able to afford to buy in the past. As a result, the vacancy rate is higher than usual among rental properties, making the rental market more competitive than ever and keeping rental rates relatively stable.

Remember, the money you save by renting can be invested. For example, if you saved $400 a month by renting rather than owning, and set it aside in a savings account with a 4 percent interest rate for 20 years, you would end up with almost $150,000.

Of course, owning a home has proven to be more profitable over the long term, but again, the investment takes time and energy. Many real estate experts say that buying a home makes sense only if you plan to live in it for three to five years. In the housing boom that kicked off the 21st century, a lot of people have made money by flipping their properties after owning for just months. But that is not the norm. When you buy and sell a home, there are costs such as real estate commission and legal fees, to name just two (more on these costs in future chapters).

For many people, owning their own home is also an achievement. This is particularly true for the growing number of single women doing it on their own. Not only is there pride of ownership, but there is the freedom to decorate according to your own tastes. It's your home now.

There is also the obvious financial advantage of building equity. You build equity not just by paying down the mortgage, but as the house appreciates over time. Of course the housing market varies from region to region (and neighbourhood to neighbourhood), and there is no guarantee you will make money if you sell, but as a general rule real estate does appreciate over time.

Can You Afford It?

Toronto realtor Brad Lamb says women have to take control of their finances and, if they are ready to buy, take action.

"What women have to stop doing is allowing the men in their lives to dictate their financial future. They have to say, 'If I'm dating a guy, or not dating a guy, or engaged to a guy, it doesn't matter. I'm going to do what I have to do and what's good for me.' That is what men do. They don't worry about it. They just go off and do what they want."

He sees more women in control of their finances than ever before, which is why more are buying real estate. "I think when women buy their own first place they are saying, 'It's okay if I'm not married. It's okay if I'm not living with someone. It's okay if I never get married. My preference might be to find that one person I can live with, but if I don't, I'm taking charge of my life.' A lot more women are doing it now than 10 years ago and it's a gigantic buying force."

- - - -

So how do you know if you can afford to buy? The common affordability rule used by financial experts is that your monthly housing costs should not be more than 32 percent of your gross household monthly income. This sounds reasonable. Remember, gross income is the amount you earn before tax. The money you actually get to spend from your pay-cheque after taxes are taken off is known as your net income.

CMHC defines monthly housing costs as your mortgage payment, as well as taxes and heating costs. If you own a condo, this sum also includes half your monthly condo fees. Add up these costs, and compare them to your gross income, and you'll have a calculation known as your "gross debt service ratio."

Here's an example. If your gross monthly income is $5,000 (you earn $60,000 a year), you should pay no more than $1,600 in monthly housing expenses ($5,000 x 32%).

The next thing to consider is your total monthly debt load. This includes car loans, credit card payments, cell phone bills, gym memberships and other monthly financial commitments. When you add these costs to that first calculation of housing costs, and compare them to your income, you'll have what's known as your "total debt service ratio." The general rule is that your total debt load should not be more than 40 percent of your monthly income. If it is, you may want to think twice about home ownership. Or, get those costs down to 40 percent or less before you buy.

Patricia Lovett-Reid, a certified financial planner and wealth management spokesperson, as well as a senior vice-president with TD Waterhouse Canada, says you have to be honest with yourself about how much money you are really spending. It's not like a diet where you can cheat when nobody is looking. "Clearly understand the money you have coming in from all sources and clearly know what you are spending your money on," Patricia says.

This rule is especially true for single women buyers, because they will be solely responsible for the finances it takes to buy and maintain a home. She advises women to know their financial situation before they start looking for a home, and especially before they visit a bank or mortgage broker to negotiate rates.

"Treat yourself as though you are the chief financial officer. Ask yourself, 'What are the risks? What will this mean for my overall lifestyle?' There is no fun in being asset rich and cash poor," says Patricia.

"People underestimate the stress and anxiety that owning a home can place on you."

– – – –

Another thing to remember is the real cost of owning a home. You hear people say that their mortgage payment is the same as rent, and that renting is equal to "throwing away money." This is not quite true.

Owning a home has many more monthly expenses than making the mortgage payment. There is property insurance, property taxes, maintenance and/or condo fees, depending on where you live. Financial experts say the extra fees can add up to 45 percent above the regular mortgage payment. I'll go into more detail on finances in Chapter Four, but here's a quick sketch of how the costs can add up:

Assume you pay $1,200 a month in rent, but you want to buy a home with a $250,000 price tag. If you put down $50,000, at an interest rate of 6 percent your mortgage payment will be about $1,280 monthly. (This example is based on a 25-year amortization and doesn't include mortgage insurance costs. More on this later.) Not too far off from what you pay in rent, right? Just wait, there's more.

Add property taxes of about $200 a month to those monthly expenses, along with at least $50 for property insurance, and at least $100 (or more, especially as fuel prices rise) for utilities such as heat and hydro. Homeowners also need to set aside costs for unexpected repairs, or even emergencies such as a flooded basement or leaky roof.

If you plan to buy a condo, you'll need to set aside money for condo fees. These fees are for expenses to maintain the common areas of the building, including insurance, window cleaning, heat, lights. Condo corporations are also required to set money aside in a reserve for any larger repairs that may be needed, such as repaving the driveway or upgrading the parking garage. Monthly condo fees can range anywhere from about

$150 (if you are really lucky) to $600 or more, depending on the age of the building and what amenities it has, such as a pool, etc.

Depending on how much you've saved up for a down payment, you might also have the additional cost of mortgage insurance. When you take out a mortgage with less than 25 percent down, you will be required (by law) to buy mortgage insurance. The amount of the premium varies between 0.65 and 2.75 percent of the total mortgage. This fee will be added on to your mortgage, and paid monthly as part of your mortgage payment. (Again, I'll give you more details on these costs and other financial matters in Chapter Four.)

So, as you can see, the extra costs of home ownership can add up.

While there are some costs of home ownership you can never recover, such as utilities and interest paid to the bank on your mortgage, you are also building equity every time you make a payment. Time itself is also your ally in equity-building, since, in most cases, your house appreciates over time.

- - - -

Still not sure that you are ready to buy? Financial experts suggest trying a six-month savings test even before you start looking for a home. To do the savings test, your first step is to figure out how much you want to spend on a home, and how those costs outlined above will break down monthly.

Assume you are renting a place for $1,200 a month, but the house you want to buy, including all expenses, will cost you about $1,700 a month. The difference is $500. For six months, set aside that extra $500 into a savings account. The idea is to see how you can handle the extra payment. If, after six months, you cannot make the payments, or setting aside that extra cash is too much added stress, it is probably not time for you to buy. On the other hand, if you were able to set aside the money with little worry, you will likely have little trouble affording that first home.

At the end of this test, no matter what the outcome, you have saved $3,000. You can spend it on a down payment—or a vacation.

You're Ready, But Not So Fast!

You've read the pros and cons of buying real estate, and believe that you are ready to buy. Hold on. There is one more hurdle you should pass before starting to house hunt: you need to get preapproved for a mortgage. This is a document from a bank (or other financial institution) stating how much you may borrow from that institution to buy a home. The amount is based on current interest rates, an assessment of your financial ability to handle the cost of a mortgage, and a check of your credit history.

This information is good to have before you start shopping for a home—it lets you know the price range you can afford to look at. Also, when the time comes to make an offer on a home you've fallen in love with, that preapproved mortgage will show the vendor that you're serious about the purchase and able to follow through. The seller doesn't have to worry that the transaction may fall through because you cannot get the financing.

It also makes you a more attractive buyer if you find yourself in a bidding war for a property. If a seller has three offers on a house, they are certain to put those with preapproved mortgages at the top of the list—sometimes even if your offer is lower. Some vendors would rather have a sure sale at a lower price than a conditional sale at a slighter higher one.

Note that preapproved is different from prequalified. Prequalified means you have a general idea of the price range you can afford. Many potential homebuyers prequalify online, using lending websites to see how much they might be able to borrow. Prequalification doesn't typically include an analysis of your credit. You also do not nail down an interest rate when you are prequalified by a lender or broker.

Prequalification is like the first date—the lender doesn't know enough about you to really make a commitment.

Preapproval, on the other hand, means the lender has gotten to know you better and has made a commitment to you. The lender takes a hard look at your financial picture before telling you if, and how much, you can borrow for a home.

Some of the things you will need to bring with you when you request mortgage preapproval include:

✓ Personal information, including identification such as a driver's licence and social insurance number

✓ Details on your job, including confirmation of salary using a recent pay stub, or a letter from your employer

✓ A list of all sources of income

✓ Information and details on all bank accounts, loans and other debts

✓ Proof of financial assets, such as your car

✓ Source and amount of down payment, deposit and closing costs (e.g., if you'll be getting money from mom and dad you need a "gift letter"; if you plan to use a work bonus, you'll need proof of the bonus from your employer, etc.)

The lender will tell you the maximum loan they will give you based on this information.

Experts recommend you don't buy any big-ticket items on credit shortly before the preapproval process. This includes leasing a new car or financing that state-of-the-art flat-screen TV. Because mortgages are based on the amount of money you pay out monthly, versus the amount you take in, any new debt can impact the results of your mortgage application.

One more thing to remember: The amount of mortgage you will qualify for is the maximum loan *the lender believes you can afford.* That doesn't necessarily mean that's *the price you should pay.* You should really leave financial room for other expenses such as renovations, if necessary—or, better yet, new furniture!

Congratulations!

You've read the pros and cons of buying. You are emotionally ready for the responsibility. You are not waiting for Mr. Right. You can afford to buy, and you have the preapproved mortgage. Congratulations, you are ready for home ownership. From here on, I will take you through all of the steps of buying a home, and warn you of the missteps. Remember, there are great rewards in owning your own home, especially as a single woman. And unlike those shoes in your closet and that car in your driveway, a home can actually increase in value over time.

Checklist: Are You Ready?

✓ Don't wait for Mr. Right. Decide instead if you are ready to buy on your own.

✓ Calculate your gross debt service ratio. Is it less than 32 percent?

✓ Calculate your total debt service ratio. Is it less than 40 percent?

✓ Understand the *real* costs of owning a home. These include the mortgage payments, as well as taxes, condo fees if they apply, and money needed to make any repairs that pop up.

✓ Try the six-month savings test to see if you can live stress-free with extra expenses.

✓ Get preapproved for a mortgage.

✓ Be prepared for extra home ownership costs.

Common Mistakes to Avoid:

✗ Waiting for Mr. Right before buying a home.

✗ Having too much debt.

✗ Not realizing the extra costs of home ownership.

✗ Not getting preapproval for a mortgage before house hunting.

2

The Perfect
Agent

*T*he next logical step in buying a home is
finding a real estate agent. Like home-buying
itself, looking for the perfect agent is a lot like
dating: you may want to meet a few of them before picking the one you actually go out with.

You've heard of (and maybe done) speed dating. This is not much
different. A smart way to begin is to get referrals from friends and family, then sit down with two or three agents and let them know what you
are looking for in the buyer-agent relationship. Remember that you
and your agent are going to spend a lot of time together. He or she will
need to know you personally—your likes and dislikes—and you will be

travelling a lot together from house to house. You want to pick an agent that you get along with, and someone you feel you can trust.

Liz, a fifty-something travel consultant, didn't have the best of luck with the first real estate agent she chose. Soon after a divorce, she decided to buy her own home. An organized person, Liz prepared a checklist.

She wanted to live in the same neighbourhood as her ex-husband because they had joint custody and one of the children was still in high school. Liz wanted a house within walking distance of the school. She also had a definite price range in mind and was resolved not to exceed it. Unfortunately, her agent didn't listen very well. He had the impression that she was rich and was low-balling her affordability range.

"I think I dress pretty well, and I wear high heels and I have this British accent, so this real estate agent showed me things I couldn't afford," says Liz. She fired him after some unsatisfactory outings—and didn't mince her words with him. "I said, 'You aren't listening to me and I just don't think this is working out between the two of us. I don't need your services anymore.'"

The next agent she tried was a woman whose husband used to be her hairdresser. "I went from a male agent to a female agent, thinking maybe a woman would listen to a woman. It is like you do with doctors; if someone has to prod you when you get to a certain age, you prefer it to be a woman."

But the theory proved to be unfounded in this case. The agent was better than the first, but not someone Liz felt comfortable working with, despite having a personal connection. In fact, the personal relationship may have been the problem. "She was slightly better, she was in the right ballpark, but I wanted someone to take me really seriously—not feel sorry for me and baby me, but to understand. It's not an easy time in anyone's life," Liz says of her post-divorce house hunting.

She dumped the second agent, too. This time, Liz did it more gently. She told the agent she was no longer interested in buying. It wasn't true, and isn't an advisable approach, but at the time it seemed to Liz like the easiest way to end the relationship.

Determined to find the perfect match, Liz got a recommendation from a friend. He was a male agent and was said to have the one main quality Liz wanted in this type of partnership: he was a good listener. It turned out to be a match. "Everything he showed me I could afford. He didn't waste my time at all. He only called when he was serious and he actually listened to me."

It didn't take Liz long to find a home after that. She bought an 85-year-old townhome in Toronto's Beach neighbourhood, right around the corner from her son's school. The house and property needed a little work, but the location, price and space were right for her.

Looking back, Liz says finding the right agent made the house hunting easier. "Make sure the real estate agent is listening to you. It's the most important piece of advice I can give anyone."

Beth, an online editor based in St. John's, Newfoundland, was in her thirties when she started looking for her first home. Her first agent was the person who actually was listing a house she was interested in buying. The relationship turned sour when she felt he pressured her into bidding on the home even though it was beyond her price range. "Once I put in an offer, I thought, 'Ohmigod, what have I got myself into?'"

Beth went to her bank. The loans manager said that while he could probably push through the mortgage because she was a good client, it would stretch her financially. Beth wanted to back out of the deal anyway, so told her banker she would not be upset if he rejected her financing request. He did. Beth then gave the bad news to the seller.

The deal was dead and Beth was relieved. She promptly fired the agent and, having been spooked by the experience, stopped looking at houses. "It's quite scary to have someone pressure you into such a big decision," Beth recalls. "Back then, I was quite naive and didn't realize that I should have an agent representing my interests. The guy was just trying to sell the property and did a hard sell with me: 'This house won't last! Make a bid now or it will be gone!' I got sucked in by that because I knew nothing about the real estate business and how the bargaining process works."

The experience taught her how important it is to have an agent you trust, especially as a single woman. Says Beth: "Being with an agent who you feel has your best interests in mind is really important when you are by yourself, because you don't have someone else to throw stuff out and discuss things with."

Later, Beth found a female agent she felt more comfortable working with. She gave the agent a price range and list of features she was looking for in a home. The agent then came back with half a dozen properties to view. "After we would go see a house, she would say to me, 'You don't want that house; it's too much work,' or she would point out what problems there were."

There was one house Beth really wanted, but the price seemed too high. It was a three-storey rowhouse in downtown St. John's that was about 90 years old. "When I walked into the house for the first time, it was late afternoon and the sun filled the first floor with light and I thought, 'This house has a great feel. It feels like home.'"

But Beth was a little daunted by the work that needed to be done on the house. Beth's agent, and her mother, walked through the home with her a second time and pointed out the potential. After some tough negotiating, Beth bought the house at a price she was willing to pay. She credits her agent for not pressuring her into making a decision, and for understanding her needs. "My agent turned out to be a great ally for me. She wasn't obsessed with getting the commission."

Beth is now married and has moved to the suburbs of St. John's. She and her husband purchased their house in a private sale, and she was able to draw on the experience of using a good agent the first time around.

Jennifer, whom you met in Chapter One, is not the type to be lured by slick salespeople. When it came time to buy, she wanted an agent she could talk to, and who wasn't turned off by her price range of about $200,000, which is low by Toronto standards. She took a referral from a friend based on the advice he was "the anti-agent."

"He drove a Volkswagen, dressed casually, was a straight shooter and about the same age as me," Jennifer recalls. "There was never any pressure to go higher in price." Jennifer also wanted an agent who could explain the home-buying process to her, since she was a first-timer. "That was important to me when I got into some of those situations where I didn't quite understand what I needed to do. He was like a therapist; he could talk me through it."

You need to make a connection when you choose your agent—again, like dating. Remember that your real estate agent doesn't just help you find listings, drive you around, and negotiate offers on your behalf. He or she needs to understand your interests.

Here are some questions industry experts suggest you should explore with a potential agent:

- How long have you been in real estate?
- What areas/neighbourhoods do you specialize in?
- Is this your full-time job?
- What part of the job do you enjoy most?
- How many home sales did you participate in last year? Price range?
- Do you normally work with sellers or buyers?
- How many buyers are you presently working with? How many sellers?
- Do you have references from buyers you've worked with in the past?

For the agent to understand your needs, he or she should also be asking questions—of you—during the first meeting. They need to know what area you want to look in and your price range. You want an agent who isn't afraid to ask you questions and who can talk straight with you. If you are a first-time home buyer, the agent should explain to you how the agent-buyer relationship works.

Shelly Smee, a Vancouver real estate agent, says a big part of her business is selling to first-time homebuyers. She says any agent who doesn't take the time to walk you through the process—whether it's your first time or you are a repeat buyer—isn't someone you should work with. "If your realtor makes you feel like an idiot because you don't know what they are talking about, say 'Thank you very much' and move on to someone else."

Toronto agent Darren Josephs (who was my agent when I bought and sold in Toronto) says he, too, tries to educate his clients about home buying. Part of this means pointing out things about each home that a buyer should know. "Agents should point out positives and negatives, whether it's an old roof, or the potential resale value of a house. I think when an agent tries to pump every house, that is when you should start to question his or her motives," Darren says.

I didn't follow much of the advice I'm giving you about finding a real estate agent when I decided it was time to buy my first home. Instead of asking for referrals, I simply called the Re/Max office around the corner from where I was living and the receptionist put me through to an agent who happened to be in the office that day. (Agents are rarely in the office and tend to live in their cars and on their cell phones.) But that's how I met Darren. He was polite (even though I sounded scattered) and asked me a few questions about location and price range. I told him what I was looking for and he promised to set aside a package of listings for me to pick up and sort through at my convenience.

I picked up the package the next day and circled a few of my favourites. One in particular caught my eye, and the price was right. I called Darren and he arranged for us to meet at the house that Saturday. I brought a friend who was curious about buying a place of her own and wondered what types of properties were out there.

While I expected to be pressured and pitched to by the agent, that didn't happen. It turned out to be a fun afternoon of not only seeing how other people lived (who isn't fascinated by other people's living spaces?), but getting invaluable information on what to look for and consider when buying a home. By the end of the afternoon I not only had my eye on the place I wanted to buy—it was that first house I saw— but I had found a great agent. When it was time to make a decision, he stood back and let me decide what was best for me. He also referred me to a smart, no-nonsense lawyer. I have since used both agent and lawyer in other home-buying and -selling situations. I have also referred my agent to about half a dozen friends and colleagues and they have been equally happy with their agent–buyer relationship. When I bought in Hamilton, I chose a well-known local brokerage firm, Judy Marsales Real Estate Ltd. I scanned the website and picked an agent from a photo who I thought looked about my age, and would represent my interests. After our first outing, I knew I had made the right decision choosing Angela Nolan—who, as you know from an earlier mention in this book, had also bought as a single woman in the past.

Toronto real estate agent Doug Heldman says referrals are a big part of the profession. "Personally, when I get a referral from a client, or from an agent in, say, Vancouver, I have an extra special commitment to ensuring the job is done properly," he says. Doug says real estate agents don't just have their own reputations to worry about. They are also often relied upon to recommend lawyers, mortgage brokers and contractors. "It's our business life, and a big part of that is previous clientele. If you think about it like inventory, as real estate agents, we don't have stock on the shelves. There is nothing on our shelves other than a database of people we've worked with in the past."

Doug says agents, in general, don't mind being interviewed by buyers. "It's good for potential buyers and for real estate agents. Real estate agents don't get along with everyone and the same thing is true in reverse."

As for the interview, Doug recommends that the buyer and agent sit down and talk about the process, including how the relationship between an agent and buyer works. He also recommends a trial period with the client—again, like dating. Some agents will ask you to sign a buyer-agent agreement, which is standard in the business. Doug recommends a 30-day trial period. "After 30 days, you should be able to communicate what is working for you, and what isn't."

If you like the agent, you should then feel comfortable signing a longer agreement, perhaps six months. Remember, the greater the commitment you give your agent, the better the relationship. But be sure you are happy with the pairing before you sign.

It's Not You—It's Me

What if you aren't happy with your agent? It's no different from ending any relationship. It's best to be up front with your agent, according to Doug. "Honesty is the best policy. The buyer is best served by saying, 'I would be much more comfortable working with someone else.' I'm not sure you need to trounce the person you are working with. It's just like dating."

Likewise, agents have the right to dump clients. Doug says an agent may decide he or she cannot meet the needs of the buyer and should let them know. "There is nothing wrong with being honest, as long as you are always being professional."

It may even be an issue of the agent not understanding the client just because they have different personalities. This happens in the workplace, with families, and sometimes with real estate agents. For instance, Doug says he may begin to work with a single woman and come to the conclusion that she would be better off working with a female agent who understands what she is looking for in a home. There is no shame in realizing you and your client are two different people, he says.

When it comes to single women buyers, Doug says, they are usually better than men at fully disclosing what they are thinking and feeling about home buying. "That serves them extremely well. It's important relationship building because a real estate agent will act on that information. That means talking in depth about your financial situation or what your fears are, such as what neighbourhoods you don't want to live in and why."

Realtor Brad Lamb, whom you also met in Chapter One, finds that single women tend to be more intimidated than men by the buying process. He says good agents respect that difference and cater to it. "Women need to get comfortable. They need to have a lot of research. They need to feel a very strong connection to their real estate agent. They also tend to listen to their real estate agent."

What's more, Brad believes women are more loyal to their agents than men. "You rarely find a man referring to a guy as their lawyer or their accountant. They have no loyalty, either way. Women, when you sit down and talk to them, will say, 'Well, I'll have to show that to my lawyer.' And they address us as their agent."

Brad says that, overall, single women make great clients, which in turn means they get great deals. "When a client listens to their agent and the agent is a good agent, they are going to do better than if they fight them. I find that is the case. Women listen more. They don't just jump into it."

Some clients do need a nudge, though, says Brad. "You find your-self saying to some of them, 'Look, forget about the money I'm going to make because it's not that much money. You've really got to look at this. You are 35 years old and you don't have a place and you make $100,000 a year and you are pissing it all away on vacations and clothes and a nice apartment that you don't own. You have to start figuring it out: When you're 65, what are you going to do?'"

That said, a good agent is also one who does not rush you. Too often, buyers feel that they've taken up too much of an agent's time and have to either stop looking, or buy something soon. A lot of my single women friends have suffered from this guilt. Just like they fear calling that new boyfriend one too many times, they fear their agent will grow tired of their indecision and eventually dump them. A good agent is one who sticks with you.

When it came to buying her most recent Toronto home, Esther, a widow in her fifties, chose an agent of the same age, thinking they would have common interests. They went to see dozens of homes, but after a while the agent became impatient. "At one point she said, 'What's wrong? They are all semis, they are all about the same,'" Esther recalls of that agent. "I thought, 'Whoa! I will know it when I see it.'"

Esther decided to find someone else to work with who wouldn't pressure her to buy. She got a referral from a friend, and this agent turned out to be more her type. "It makes a big difference," she says, "the amount of pressure that people put on you." She also appreci-ated that the new agent didn't inundate her with properties that were not in her price range.

After months of searching, Esther finally found a home with a garden in a lovely neighbourhood north of downtown. She credits her patient agent for taking her through the house-hunting process. Her advice: "Talk to the person and make sure you have the same goals and really list what you want. Have a clear idea of what you want. Do not get pressured into going into a price range you cannot afford."

Buying from a Floor Plan

With the building boom across Canada, a lot of buyers are purchasing houses and condos from floor plans. In this circumstance, you visit a showroom and, if you want to buy a place, you put down a deposit and follow a payment schedule until your new place is ready for you. You don't necessarily need to use a real estate agent in this instance. In fact, the builder would prefer you didn't use an agent because it's one less person the builder has to pay. (You will, of course, need the services of your real estate lawyer for the transaction and general guidance.) Having an agent comes in handy here, though, because even if price isn't negotiable, you can often negotiate upgrades. Remember, as celebrity real estate mogul Donald Trump says, "Negotiate everything."

What's more, an agent who has acted for buyers and sellers of newly built homes can advise you on a number of aspects of the transaction. And, having advised other new-house buyers, might even be able to help you visualize what the floor plans will look like in real life.

I bought my third property from a builder's floor plan. It was an old boiler factory that was being converted into 11 lofts. My agent, Darren, not only helped me negotiate the sale but also recommended a sliding "barn" door between the bedroom and living room to let in more light. It became one of that unit's best features. Also, at one point, the builder tried to take away my rooftop deck and offered to throw in stainless-steel appliances as an upgrade instead. Darren helped me negotiate. He advised me that private outdoor space has a much higher resale value than appliances—no matter how shiny. In the end, the deck remained.

Going It Alone

You *can* buy a house without an agent, but it means doing a lot of work yourself. That includes finding the listings, researching neighbourhoods and market prices for the area, arranging showings and doing your own negotiating. Remember that, as a home *buyer,* using a real estate agent does not cost you money. The commission for the sale of a home is paid for by the *seller,* also known as the *vendor.*

Commission can range from about 4 to 6 percent of the selling price, depending on where you live, and how good the seller's negotiating skills are. In most cases, the buying and selling agents split the commission. An exception may be if the seller has negotiated a lower commission—let's say 4.5 percent—the buying agent will get 2.5 percent and the selling agent will get 2 percent. This means, as a home buyer, your agent will get paid his or her full percentage of the commission no matter what price the home sells for. There can, of course, be exceptions to this example.

You can work with the agent who is selling the house, but remember that agent is working for the seller. It is their job to get the seller the best price possible, not you. In some cases, the seller's agent may agree to lower the overall commission if they are "double-ending"—that is, acting for both the buyer and seller. For instance, the agent representing the seller may agree to charge a 3-percent commission if the house is sold to a buyer he or she also represents. The advantage for you, the buyer, is that the seller may agree to lower the selling price of the house because the seller is paying a smaller commission.

However, this is a big "if." As a buyer, you are not privy to the commission arrangement made between the seller and his or her agent. In most cases, it is best to find your own agent, who can negotiate the best price possible for you.

Also remember that the seller (and their agent) has a legal obligation to tell you about any serious problems with the home. Upon selling, in most jurisdictions, the seller must fill out a form in which he or she is asked to disclose a number of details about the property, including any potential problems such as a leaky roof or basement. But be aware that there is also a "don't know" choice the seller can check off in this disclosure document, which can sometimes be used to hide problems. If, after you've bought the home and you find the basement is leaking, for instance, you can try to hold the seller accountable for not disclosing this information. However, it may be difficult to prove. If you discover the problem after the deal is closed, you may have to go to court to fight to have the problem fixed, which could be more costly than simply paying for the repair yourself. This is why it's a good idea to have a home inspection, so you can find out about any potential problems with the home before the deal is done.

Another advantage to finding your own agent is that they have access to the majority of listings before they go online. Agents receive alerts of new listings about 24 to 48 hours before they are listed on mls.ca. If you are working with an agent, and they know what type of property you are looking for, they may see a suitable property on this list and get this listing to you sooner than if you'd found it online yourself. The same scenario applies if a property that you have had your eye on suddenly drops in price.

There is one other scenario you may come across when using an agent. It's known as a dual agency agreement. This means that your agent, and the agent selling the home you want to buy, are from the same broker. If this happens, the company has to disclose to you, in writing, that they represent both sides of the agreement.

Real Estate Agents Are People, Too

You've heard about bad agents who have used pressure tactics, or have been too pushy, but what about bad clients? They are out there.

In interviewing agents for this book, I have heard some terrible stories of agents being mistreated by clients. In one case, a first-time buyer (a woman) in Toronto had been working for months with her agent. He showed her dozens of properties, driving her across the city from house to house. One day, while the agent was in the hospital awaiting emergency surgery, she called to tell him about a house she wanted to buy. It had been on the market for weeks, which meant it was not about to sell anytime soon. The agent, in a conversation with her from the hospital two hours before he was to go under the knife, said he would get a colleague to show her the property the next morning.

She never called back. For weeks, the agent tried to reconnect with his client, until he learned she had in fact bought that property—using the seller's agent. He received nothing for his months of hard work.

Remember that agents are people, too. They are doing a job. Agents make money on commission from home sales, but they also pay their own expenses, from licensing and marketing fees to transportation and administration costs. These fees can add up to roughly 40 percent of their income, before tax. If you are unhappy with your agent, let him or her go *after* you have fulfilled your side of the agreement. Read the agreement thoroughly before you sign it, understand its implications, and honour them. When you hire an agent, you should give the same respect you demand from them.

Living Happily Ever After

The buyer-agent relationship is the most important one in the home-buying process. You need someone who "gets you," and with whom you can share personal information. "It really is similar to dating," says realtor Brad Lamb. "You have to be comfortable in the relationship. You are going to have an intense, short-term relationship with this person and you are going to need to trust them implicitly. You are also going to be under more pressure than you've ever been in your life, and you are going to feel it."

Remember, your agent is the person who will introduce you to that perfect home you've been saving for so long to buy. Be sure the relationship is one that works for you.

Checklist: What to Look For in an Agent

✓ Someone you feel comfortable with.

✓ Someone who understands your home-buying needs, including taste, location and price range.

✓ Someone who knows the area in which you want to buy.

✓ Someone with strong references from previous clients.

Common Mistakes to Avoid:

✗ Staying with a bad agent. Do not feel obligated to do so.

✗ Letting an agent pressure you into buying. If you need a second opinion, talk to your lawyer or mortgage lender.

✗ Staying with an agent who doesn't listen to you about your house-hunting needs.

✗ Using the seller's agent for convenience and not ending up with a satisfactory house or a satisfactory deal.

3

Location, Location, *Location*

$\mathcal{W}$hat if you found the perfect house—right size, right price, popular neighbourhood— but there was a down-at-the-heels rooming house next door? Would you buy it and put up with the transient neighbours? How about a fabulous loft space on a street surrounded by several homeless shelters?

It's one of the oldest clichés in the real estate advice books, but "location, location, location" really is very important when it comes to buying a home. It doesn't matter how perfect you think that home is you've found, a bad location can crush your home ownership dreams.

This is one of the toughest lessons I learned when buying my first home. Oh, yes, and my third one. Bad neighbours and bad neighbourhoods—I've bought near both. (There is a reason I'm writing this book!) More on my location mistakes and how you can avoid them later in this chapter. I'll also talk here about important location considerations for single women, such as safe neighbourhoods, personable neighbours, and adequate space. But first things first: You need to figure out what you want in a home. Make a list—just like the one you drew up in trying to find the perfect partner (admit it, you've done this). You need to figure out what's important to you in a future home.

- - - -

Christiane, a thirty-something manager at a Toronto-based book publisher, bought a home in Port Credit, Ontario, a small town west of Toronto. She had a list of criteria for her first home, including what she could afford as a single woman, which is why she started looking beyond Toronto's downtown core.

"I didn't want to be in a subdivision and I didn't want to live in a cookie-cutter neighbourhood where all of the houses are jammed together, and it had to have trees," says Christiane. "I wanted a neighbourhood with some history, but somewhere close to the QEW highway to commute to work."

The list didn't end there. She also wanted a house without a garage, and a big yard. Also the size of the house had to be just right. "I wanted a house that suited me as a single person. I didn't want a house that was so big I would feel like I was rattling around in it. I didn't want the house to accentuate my singledom. It had to be big enough to have friends over, but small enough so I wouldn't get lost in it." It also had to be near a park, the lake, and amenities she could walk to such as the store, the pub and a few retail shops.

Finally, it had to be newly renovated. "I didn't want the pain and surprise of finding out a few months after moving in that I needed a new roof," says Christiane. "And I wasn't interested in renovating. I fear getting taken by contractors, especially since I don't have anyone in my family to give me advice on those types of things."

After nearly giving up hope, Christiane did find a home with all the qualities on her list. It was an evening in September 2003 when weather forecasters had warned of a rainstorm about to roll through town. Parents were racing to pick their children up from school to avoid the dangerous weather, while Christiane was in the car with her agent, who persuaded her to look at one last property that day—a new listing that she would be the first to see. She was reluctant, but decided to go along with the suggestion.

"I had been looking for two months already and was rejecting everything, nothing felt right," she recalls. "I was waiting for that feeling I kept hearing about, but I wasn't getting it." Then she walked into the place in Port Credit. "The minute I walked in the front door I was in love," she says. "It felt right. It felt like I belonged here."

She paid asking price for the home, and calls her decision to wait and buy the place she wanted "the best decision I've ever made."

House or Condo?

First, decide what type of home you want. Your choice begins with—but isn't limited to—whether you want a house or a condo. If you're opting for a house, do you want a detached house, semi-detached (you share one common wall with the house next door), or a townhouse or rowhouse (you share walls on both sides of your house, unless you live at the end of the row).

Detached homes are the most private and quiet, which is why they are often the most expensive. The bigger price tag could be worth it if you can't live with other people's noise (or if you're a music lover and want to shake the walls once in a while).

Remember, though, as I mentioned in an earlier section on renting versus buying, any home—whether attached or detached—requires regular maintenance. You need to think about whether your busy life includes time for a little handywoman work, as well as cleaning eavestroughs, mowing the lawn and shovelling snow off the sidewalk.

Condo ownership demands less effort from you in terms of maintenance, but you pay for it in the form of a monthly condo fee. Among other things, the fee covers the cost of someone else to shovel snow, cut grass, and clean the common areas and hallways.

Natalie, the thirty-something journalist with the downtown Toronto condo, says that, for her, the fees are worth the money. "As a single woman I don't have the time to take care of all those little things. A house is a lot of work. I would rather go to the local coffee shop and read or write and drink my coffee than worry about shovelling snow."

"Wow, this space is huge—or is it?"

Many single women choose condos because the space is sufficient for one. The smaller quarters also make condo ownership more affordable. Here are some questions to consider when looking for the right size space for you:

- How many bedrooms do you need?
- Do you need an office/study room?
- How much storage space/closet space do you need?
- Do you need a parking spot?
- Do you have room for your pet(s)?
- Do you want a gym/pool nearby (or in the building)?
- Do you need a park/running trails nearby?

- Do you need space for overnight guests? If so, you may want an extra bedroom, and possibly guest parking.

If you have pets and are considering buying a condo, be sure to check the condo's bylaws and ensure that pets are permitted. Many condos have strict rules on pets. Some don't allow them, period; others allow only small dogs or cats and often a condo owner is restricted to one pet. The last thing you want to find out after you've bought a home is that you cannot bring along your dog or cat. Both of you will be heartbroken.

New or Resale?

The first house I bought was resale. It had character, and I could afford it. I didn't even look at new homes, since I imagined new spaces to be sterile and not very cozy.

The second home I bought was also a resale, but it had been newly renovated. It was freshly painted and new carpets and kitchen appliances had been installed. Once I added my own furniture, I felt very comfortable. It was home. I was a renovation convert.

The third home I bought, the retrofitted loft in an old factory building, was also entirely new on the inside. What's more, the fixtures were modern—granite countertops, slate floors. Suddenly, I couldn't remember what was so special about a resale!

New or resale? It really comes down to personal choice. A lot of people who buy new do it for the convenience, and are often willing to pay a premium for it, while others buy resale so they can do their own renovations to suit their tastes. On the next page there is a list of pros and cons of new versus resale from the Canada Mortgage and Housing Corporation.

New Home: Pros

- Personalized choices. You may be able to upgrade or choose certain items such as siding, flooring, cabinets, plumbing and electrical fixtures.
- Built to the latest codes/standards. For example, the most recent structural, electrical and energy-efficiency standards will be applied.
- Lower maintenance costs. These are typically lower because everything is new and many items are covered by warranty.
- Builder's warranty usually applies. A homebuilder's warranty is available in all provinces (except Nunavut and the Northwest Territories). Having a warranty to cover the cost of a breakdown in a major system, such as plumbing, air conditioning or heating, is very important when the new owner is digging deep to cover the mortgage and taxes. (This warranty does not apply if you build the home yourself.)

New Home: Cons

- Neighbourhood amenities such as schools, shopping malls and other services may not be built for years.
- Taxes such as the Goods and Services Tax (GST) or, in certain provinces, the Harmonized Sales Tax (HST) will apply. However, you may qualify for a rebate of part of the GST or HST on homes that cost less than $450,000. For more information about the GST New Housing Rebate program, visit the Canada Revenue Agency website at http://www.cra-arc.gc.ca.
- Extra costs. You may have to shell out if you want to add a fireplace, plant trees and sod, or pave your driveway. Make sure you know exactly what's included in the price of your home. Be sure to consult with your lawyer when he or she is reviewing the purchase agreement.

Resale Home: Pros

- Easy access to services. Schools, shopping malls and other services, such as public transit, will be established in mature neighbourhoods.
- Landscaping is usually mature and fences have usually been erected. Previously owned homes may have extras such as fireplaces, finished basements or swimming pools.
- Tax break. You don't have to pay the GST/HST unless the house has been renovated substantially, and then the taxes are applied as if it were a new house.

Resale Home: Cons

- Possible redecorating and renovations required. You may need to redecorate, renovate or do major repairs such as replacing the roof, windows and doors.

(Source: Canada Mortgage and Housing Corp. www.cmhc.ca)

While I was eventually swayed by the shiny features of new homes, there are disadvantages to being the first to open the front door of a new home, especially in a new condo or housing development. One is that you don't know who your neighbours are until you move in. And, once you do move in, you may have to put up with the noise and construction that continues until the housing or condo project is complete.

I learned this lesson after selling my Toronto loft. I took a short-term rental in a brand-new condominium high-rise on the city's lakefront. The view was stunning, and being the first to use the new appliances was a treat. Less fun were the 3 a.m. fire alarms that went off almost weekly for the first month after I moved in. There was also the inconvenience of the maintenance checks to ensure that the ventilation system was functioning, that the patio met safety standards, or to fix small problems such as missing fixtures or new but faulty plumbing.

The advantage with a resale property is that many quirks have already been worked out of the home. Older resale homes also often have more character. The downside, of course, is that they have been around longer and require more maintenance, such as a new roof, furnace or garage door opener. As well, older condos often require higher condo fees as the building ages and the costs of making those repairs rises over the long term.

Get to Know Your Builder

When you buy a resale home it's recommended you try to find out some facts about the seller—to help you negotiate price. The same rule applies for buying new, only now you need to get to know the builder.

Remember that when you buy a new home you aren't just buying the space, you are also paying for the experience and commitment of the company building it. That's why choosing the right builder is important. Just as you did for your real estate agent, you'll want to get some references from the builder. Look into other projects they've done and if you can, talk to people who live in those homes.

Checking up on the builder's past projects is particularly important in a hot housing market when new construction is booming. To capitalize on the most recent housing construction craze, a lot of new companies have been born. That doesn't mean all new builders are bad, but you should find out more about their past work before signing on to one of their projects.

Here are some questions to ask when considering a builder and its project:

- "Is home building your profession?" Home building is a serious business. It takes commitment to keep up with everything that is going on in the industry. It requires solid business skills and a track record of satisfied clients. If a "builder" proposes to build your home part-time, you should proceed with caution. If this builder offers you a "better" financial deal, you need to wonder—the old adage that you get what you pay for holds true for home buying as well.

- "What is your experience, and how long have you been in business?" Good builders are proud of their track record, whether they have been in business for 3 or 30 years. They will tell you about their background, their training and experience, their strengths and what sets them apart from others. They will be honest with you about what they can do for you, when and for how much.

- "Are you a member of the Canadian Home Builders' Association (CHBA)?" Membership in this association is an indication of a builder's commitment to the industry, to the success of their own company and, ultimately, to their customers. Members agree to a code of ethics that calls for fair and honest dealings with consumers.

- "Are you a member of a home warranty program?" Warranty programs provide additional protection for the home buyer's investment. In some regions, a variety of warranties is available. Ask the builder to explain the details—you want the warranty that best meets your needs, for both the short term and the long.

- "Will you give us references from past clients?" Don't just take the builder's word for it. Contact past customers to find out how satisfied they are with their new home. Ask if the home was completed on budget and on time, what the builder was like to work with (easy to talk with, understanding, helpful), and about the company's after-sales service.

continued

- "What after-sales service does your company provide?" Professional builders stand behind their homes with an after-sales service program. Ask the builder to explain the program in some detail: what's covered, how to request service and the typical response time.

- "Can we visit your work site(s)?" The work site offers many clues about the company and the quality of the builder's homes. Ask for a conducted tour of a home under construction and a chance to meet the site crew. Take note of the details: is the site clean and orderly, are materials stored out of the weather, and so on.

Ask as many questions as you like and choose a builder you feel comfortable working with.

Source: Canadian Home Builders' Association

Miss Fix It?

Trish Greene, a realtor based in St. John's, Newfoundland, says many of her single women clients make the mistake of only looking at the cosmetics of a house, and not understanding the nature and extent of repairs that have to be done to properly maintain a property.

"They look for 'pretty,' and pretty isn't always the best way to buy a house," says Trish. "Very often I have to remind them that the walls might be painted an attractive colour, but the wiring is old. The roof is old. The buyer cannot just look at the colour of the walls."

Barb, a thirty-something graphic designer, sold her new Toronto townhouse in June 2005 and moved to a farmhouse on half an acre of land in Georgetown, Ontario. "Before, I would only buy new so that I didn't have to fix anything. And, to be honest, I would suggest the same thing to most women. Now I'm in a 45-year-old house and going crazy renovating. I love it, but I'm at a different stage in life."

Barb says new homes are less work but have less mystery—a drawback if you like mystery. "In a new house you don't hear the creaking sounds, so you don't get scared at night. You are pretty well guaranteed you won't have to replace your roof, furnace or anything big. You just get to play and decorate. That's a big thing for a woman, I think. You just put up the pictures; you don't have to do all the maintenance stuff."

In her farmhouse, Barb has had to replace the septic system and had run the well dry many times before she learned how to fix it on her own. "I knew the house needed a lot of work. The guy who owned it before me was a do-it-yourselfer, but I think he really didn't know what he was doing."

Ruth, an artist over the age of 40, says she looked for a house that needed some renovations when she moved from her Toronto condo to a home in Hamilton, Ontario. The main reason was that homes in need of repair are less expensive to purchase. Ruth renovated a big section of her house, and did a lot of the work on her own. She tore down walls and put up new drywall, and stripped floors. She admits that a male friend helped her fix the plumbing, but she chose a house that required renovations she was mostly able to tackle on her own. "I like to fix stuff up, but not to the point where I'm hiring outside contractors to do all the work."

Safe and Sound

For a single woman, location is also important for safety reasons. You want to feel comfortable walking down the street by yourself—day and night—without looking over your shoulder.

Adriana, a television producer in her thirties, says safety was the main reason she bought a sixth-floor condo in downtown Toronto's St. Lawrence Market district. It has a 24-hour concierge and an access card with a panic button she can use to alert security if she feels any anxiety when nearing the building. The unit also has its own security system.

"Condo living overall was really a choice not just about living in a certain kind of aesthetic, but about safety," Adriana says. "Call me a bit paranoid, but I wanted to ensure that, since I live alone, I live in a space that's high enough above ground that someone can't try to break in from a balcony door. I have a perhaps irrational fear of that. I feel very safe at night where I am." After living in the 200-unit building for more than two years, Adriana says she hasn't heard of even one case of theft.

Living downtown also makes some women feel safe. While that may sound strange to anyone who lives in the country, single women in urban centres know it can be true.

"I want to go outside my door, go for a walk, and feel like there are a lot of people around," says Natalie, whom you heard from earlier. What's more, she says living downtown usually means living near other single friends. The married ones with kids often move to the suburbs, and as a consequence spend less time with their single girlfriends.

But safety is not just about the neighbourhood, it's also a factor in the layout of the home. Dayna, a thirty-something corporate lawyer, says a big selling feature for her downtown Vancouver townhouse was the attached garage. She believes it's much safer than having to park in an underground garage. "When I walked in and saw that feature [the attached garage], I really liked it. You pull in and you are in the house. You don't feel like someone could be waiting to attack you. That was a very attractive feature for me."

Safety means different things to different people, but it still rates as one of the main factors for single women when choosing a location. "There are all different types of women," says Toronto realtor Brad Lamb. "There are women who are very adventurous and want to live in a warehouse space in a back alley on the ground floor. They just think that is kind of cool and part of what they see themselves being. And there are other women who are more 'Daddy's girls,' and Daddy comes along and says, 'You aren't living on the ground floor. It's not happening!' And they go off and find a more comfortable place."

Neighbours can be part of the safety equation too. While they may be nosey, they can also look out for you—which is especially important for a single woman living alone. Kathy, a fifty-something employee with the City of Toronto, recommends that single women homeowners make friends with their neighbours. Kathy has three neighbours she trusts so much that they have keys to her house in case of an emergency. "If they saw someone walking out with my television, they would say something," Kathy says. "My home gives me a great sense of emotional security. Nothing bad happens to me in my house."

Up Close and Personal: Neighbours

As I hinted at early in this chapter, location is also about who lives next door. Renters may or may not care about who lives in the neighbourhood. Homeowners, generally speaking, do. Homeowners are longer-term and may become friends or at least tolerable neighbours.

Having good neighbours is a blessing for any homeowner. Not only can they add to your safety, they may also have recommendations for good contractors and plumbers, and—if you are interested—whether the guy delivering your mail is married or not. They may also have husbands you can borrow if removing the dead mouse from behind the fridge makes you squeamish. Speaking of borrowing, Kathy (the City of Toronto employee) says she has borrowed a number of items from her neighbours, but knows where to draw the line. "My rule is that if you have to borrow something three times, you need to buy one of your own."

But if good neighbours are a blessing, nightmare neighbours can make home ownership feel like a trap—because you're stuck with them. Before you make your purchase, try to introduce yourself to the neighbours and chat with them. My awful experience with neighbours happened when I bought my first property, at age 30. It was an old row-house on a side street near Toronto's trendy Queen Street West neighbourhood. When I bought it, the place seemed perfect: in my price range and needing not much more than a cosmetic makeover. What I didn't take into consideration were the neighbours. Big mistake!

The movers had not even unloaded all my furniture when I heard a fight between two men next door. The walls shook. My heart sank. In the days and months that followed, there was more noise, more fights, and a lot of parties. Walking home late one night from work, a man stopped me on my street asking for directions to a place that sounded, from his description, like a rooming house. It was then I realized the house he was looking for was the noisy one next to mine. It took multiple calls to the police and the involvement of city hall to get that noise to stop. The only problem then was that the unruly neighbours next door knew it was me who had complained. Instead of noise, I suffered weeks of jeers from the skinheads and wannabe rock stars (their band played in their backyard) who slummed it next door.

I sold that house for a good profit less than a year later, not to escape the noise, but because I needed to relocate for a job. That said, in hindsight, had I spent more time investigating the neighbourhood, and in particular the neighbours, I may have thought twice about putting in the offer in the first place.

I also had noise issues in the new loft I bought in downtown Toronto—also known as home No. 3. Because the property was new—and my neighbour's unit was worth about $85,000 more than my modest space—I didn't think noise would be a problem. As it turned out, the Bay Street bachelor liked to have parties starting at 2 a.m. He used the long hallway with the wall adjoining my bedroom as a luge-like runway surface for him and his friends to slide along after a few too many Johnny Walkers. Eventually he moved to Las Vegas, where he undoubtedly found a party atmosphere more consistent with his own, but the noise made my life miserable for many months.

If you are thinking about buying a condo, you may have multiple neighbours to consider, such as those who live in a building next to, or across from, yours. Does your window look directly into theirs? If so, that sunny room you love may wind up being darkened with closed curtains to thwart Peeping Toms. If you're looking at a condo in a building beside a vacant piece of land, consider what might be erected beside you. If it's another condo tower, your amazing view could be short-lived. These are all things to consider carefully when looking for a home.

Something Smells in Here...

When you go searching for your home, don't forget to smell around. Don't be fooled by the vanilla candles burning at the open house. What does the place really smell like after the hours of 2 to 4 p.m.?

Some neighbourhoods suffer from not-so-nice scents. In Toronto, Beach residents suffer due to pungent odours from the wastewater treatment plant, while trendsetters in King West Village cannot escape the odours emanating from the local rendering plant.

Jennifer, a thirty-something marketing manager in Toronto, says smells were important to her when buying her first home. "I didn't want the hallway smelling like someone else's dinner." She made this clear to her agent. Whenever they walked into a condo building and she smelled something she didn't like, they would leave, without even seeing the unit.

To avoid nasty surprises, spend some time in your desired neighbourhood at different times of the day. Sniff around. Of course, not all bad smells can be avoided, but it's best to know how much of a stench you may have to deal with before you make that offer to purchase.

Resale Potential

Buying a home with a strong resale value is an important consideration. Many first-time buyers make the mistake of thinking they will live in that home forever. It could happen, but if you are a single woman you may wind up marrying and/or having a partner later in life. You may also remain single but want to change neighbourhoods as you get older. Being in a hip urban spot is fine when you're in your twenties and thirties, but may grow tiresome in your forties and fifties. Here are some factors to consider when it comes to resale.

The 'hood

The closer you are to the centre of your neighbourhood, the better for resale. This means proximity to the coffee shops, grocery stores, gas station and dry cleaner. Convenience is key. And while you don't want to live on top of a major roadway, close proximity to one will be attractive to the next buyers. After all, isn't that one of the things you like about it?

"Up and coming" areas

Neighbourhoods that are already established—you know the ones, they usually have a Starbucks and a high-end clothing store along the main strip—are almost always more expensive to live in, compared to the "up and coming" areas. But paying less for the lower-valued neighbourhoods may not save you money in the long run. Toronto agent Doug Heldman says if gentrification of a neighbourhood takes a long time, say 15 years, you may get a better return if you bought, and then sold, in a better area: values tend to go up more quickly in higher-end areas. Of course, living in the better neighbourhood could mean its services, such as gas and groceries, may be more expensive.

Schools and government services

As a single woman, the last thing you should pay attention to is the school system in your area, right? Wrong. When you sell the property, many of your potential buyers will be interested in the local school system. Remember Liz, the travel consultant in Chapter Two who had to find a place near her son's school after she and her husband divorced? Don't turn your nose up at those playgrounds just yet. Nearby libraries and community centres are also good for resale.

Time out for taxes

Property taxes may be higher from one end of the city to the next. Higher taxes are usually found in those busy areas with more amenities and well-maintained roads. This is the tradeoff for buying in those better neighbourhoods. Regardless, taxes are a huge monthly outlay for many people; so bear that in mind not only for your own financial health, but for the person you could be selling your property to in future.

Location Lowdown

As you can see, picking the right location is more than just liking the home and its surrounding area. It is unlikely that you will be able to get everything you put down on your location checklist, but knowing what you want helps narrow your search. It also helps you make a smart financial decision based on your individual needs and wants.

Shelly Smee, the Vancouver realtor, says first-time homebuyers should be realistic about what they are buying. "Your first home is not going to be your dream home. You have to get a reality check. You may not be in the ideal neighbourhood. You may not have all the things you want in the home. Remember, it's your first property."

Checklist: What Do You Want in a Home?

✓ House or condo?

✓ New or used?

✓ Does it satisfy your space needs?

✓ Does the property promise good resale value?

✓ Is it in a safe location?

✓ Is it in a desirable neighbourhood that offers the promise of good neighbours?

Common Mistakes to Avoid:

✗ Not correctly estimating how much space you really need.

✗ Buying a place you cannot afford to renovate because you're overextended financially.

✗ Locating in an undesirable area because you got a "deal," leaving you with the problem of selling the property down the road.

✗ Not checking out the neighbours—they may not be a good match and could negatively impact your living experience.

✗ Buying in an unsafe area.

4

Your

Finances

*A*ttention shoppers: Remember all those outfits, shoes and other "necessities" you've been charging to your credit card? Congratulations—turns out you've been doing yourself a favour.

What you've been doing is building a credit history. This is a good thing, especially if you have been paying off that debt. It means you have proven to the lending gods that you can be trusted in borrowing money. All of that spending has been a warm-up for the biggest borrowing binge you will ever have—a mortgage.

If you haven't been as well behaved with your plastic and other debt, expect to sit in credit purgatory until you can prove your credit worthiness. Either you won't get that mortgage, or you will have to pay much higher rates than your friends who didn't dodge the monthly credit card bills.

Angela, the Hamilton realtor, says she was always very good at paying her bills on time. She didn't even use a credit card. "I thought I was being a good girl by buying everything with cash, but I kind of messed myself up. It's important that you do establish a credit history."

Once Angela realized that she needed to build that credit history, she started using plastic—and promptly paying it off. Still, she said the banks weren't very receptive to her in the early 1990s when she wanted to take out a mortgage on her own. Part of that may have been that she didn't have a long credit history, but Angela also believes banks weren't as accustomed to women buying on their own back then. "Today they fight for your business, whereas back then you had to basically beg them to get a mortgage. Consumers are also getting a lot more knowledgeable so the lenders have to do more to woo you. I think that's because more single women than men are buying houses today."

Your Credit Rating

Before you try to browbeat a banker or mortgage broker for the best rate, find out more about your credit history. Two popular sources for this information in Canada are: TransUnion (www.transunion.ca) or Equifax (www.equifax.ca). You can obtain your credit reports for free if you're willing to wait, or pay a reasonable fee for immediate online credit reports.

The credit reports give you a list of all companies from which you have applied for credit in your lifetime. This includes bank credit cards, credit unions and retailers—any and all companies that have given you money or products that you agreed to pay for later. This credit history shows if you paid your bills on time, if your account was sent to a collection agency, and if you ever declared bankruptcy. The report also shows your personal identification (name, address, social insurance number); anyone who has requested a copy of your credit file in the past three years (i.e. if you applied for a credit card); and details of your credit transactions.

Your credit is judged on what lending agencies often call the "Five C's" of credit.

- **Character:** The general impression you make on the potential lender. The lender looks at your credit and job history, education and how long you have lived in your current residence to form an opinion on whether it trusts you to repay the loan.
- **Collateral:** The bank needs to feel secure that the property you are buying is marketable if, for some reason, you cannot pay the loan. A real estate appraisal will determine the property value, including deficiencies that may impact resale. (More on appraisals later in this chapter.)
- **Capital:** How much money are you putting down to buy the house? The larger the down payment, the more likely you are to meet the mortgage payments. It also includes your ability to save money and accumulate assets such as a car. The higher your net worth, the more you have as a cushion to repay the mortgage.
- **Credit:** The bank looks at your credit history, which includes how well you paid your bills over the last six years. This includes credit cards, car loans and other credit payments. Any missed payments show up on your credit rating, which can impact your ability to get a mortgage, or the rate you received.
- **Capacity:** Considered the most important of the five factors. The lender needs to know how you will repay the loan, taking into consideration how much money you earn, how stable your job is, and

other sources of income. Also, are the monthly mortgage costs less than or equal to 32 percent of your total monthly income?

A common mistake among single women, long before they consider buying a home, is not realizing how important their credit score will be to them some day. "It can affect your whole life," says Vancouver real estate agent Shelly Smee. "The fact is that if you have more than one department store card and you do not pay it in full, or have a rotating balance, you are really hurting yourself."

Her advice: "Get rid of all department store credit cards. You want to be able to get the best mortgage rate possible. Whether you are making $50,000 or $150,000 a year, your money is your money and it should work for you—not you for it."

Shelly tries to wring this type of financial information out of her clients before they start seriously looking for a home. If they haven't been prequalified for a mortgage (see Chapter One and more later in this chapter) she requests they see a bank or mortgage broker and get that done. Potential buyers should get "financially fit" before they buy, though she acknowledges that this isn't always easy to do alone. "When I'm working with buyers, and in particular single women, it can be more challenging without that extra, second income to help pay the bills."

Still, Shelly says women should not hold off for that second income. She says recent house price history shows waiting for Mr. Right if you can afford to buy has not been wise. "Making your own financial decisions means you never have to be dependent on someone else for having that basic housing need taken care of," says Shelly. "Relationships come and go, even homes come and go, but I think a lot of women make the mistake of waiting for the perfect relationship to complete the idea of what a home is for them. Instead, women should be taught at an early age what saving is so they can make good financial decisions later in life."

Bank or Broker?

There is a great debate when you get a mortgage whether to go directly to a bank, or to a mortgage broker. A lot of people in the industry recommend independent mortgage brokers because they are not affiliated with a particular bank.

Mortgage brokers act as a conduit between borrowers and lenders. The brokers typically get paid a finder fee by the lender. The service is free to you, and the broker shops around to several lenders to get you the best rate. That said, if you have a poor credit record, you may be required to pay a fee to the broker. The common wisdom is that brokers are better for homebuyers because they focus on one thing: finding you the best mortgage rate. Banks, on the other hand, are sometimes said to be less focussed because they handle mortgages, mutual funds and other investment products.

Sheena, a thirty-something business development manager for a major Canadian retailer, says she went to a bank to see what mortgage rate they could offer, but left feeling more confused than when she came in. "They talk in their own lingo and they understand it, but they forget they are dealing with someone for whom finance is another language. My head was spinning. The bottom line is they could not beat what the mortgage broker was offering," Sheena says.

Personally, I have worked directly with a bank for each of my three mortgages, and have been happy. While I did contact a broker in the beginning, I found my bank was willing to match any rate mostly because I had a long-term relationship with them.

If you do choose a mortgage broker, check that they have the proper credentials. The Canadian Institute of Mortgage Brokers and Lenders (www.cimbl.ca) has information for consumers on ethics and standards for mortgage brokers. Most brokers are member of this association, and of their provincial association as well. Have the broker give you names and numbers of clients they've worked with. You should also talk to more than one broker at first. Just like you did with your real estate agent, you want to interview a few brokers before choosing which one to use.

Jennifer, whom you've come to know in this book, fired her first mortgage broker, a woman, who was recommended to her by a financial advisor. The broker used Jennifer's former status as a contract employee to prevent her from getting a cheaper rate, and even suggested she may not qualify for a mortgage at all. The broker also insisted on running a credit check on Jennifer's ex-boyfriend, because they had had a common law relationship. Jennifer was flabbergasted, especially since the two had broken up more than a year before. To add insult to injury, the broker was also pressuring Jennifer to make a decision because she (the broker) was about to go on vacation with her family. Jennifer was convinced she could do better. She ignored the pressure tactics and consulted a second broker to see what rate he could offer.

In the end, she got a better rate from the second broker, and a mouthful from the first one. "Her attitude was that I owed her something," Jennifer says of the first broker she consulted. "But at the end of the day the biggest thing I learned was that it isn't personal. I know she worked hard, but if her mortgage rate is higher—well, that is going to cost me thousands of dollars over the years. She wasn't happy."

Looking back, Jennifer advises anyone looking for a mortgage not to be intimidated. "The thing that really struck me about getting that mortgage is the amount of grief I went through. How many other people go through that and don't have the personality to fight back? Another thing I learned is that you can use multiple brokers. I did well, but I would definitely be much wiser going into it the next time around." However, please note that going to multiple brokers can impact your credit score.

Michelle Watson says she got her first mortgage from a bank. She felt pressured to make the decision immediately, and without being given a chance to read the fine print. Put off by the experience, but intrigued by the profession, Michelle later became a mortgage broker—specializing in mortgages for single women, no less. She now advises single women (and all her clients) to demand an explanation of all details on a mortgage application. "It's important to say 'Hold on, I would like to read the fine print!' Even if it means sitting in front of that bank official and taking up all their time and querying them about certain terms and asking the 'What ifs?' It's your money and you control it," Michelle says.

It's important to remember that the bank makes a lot of money off your mortgage over the years. Take your time—and theirs—and be sure you understand everything about your potential mortgage. You're paying for that time.

How Much Home Can You Afford?

Natalie, whom you met earlier, cautions other single women that owning a home on your own, especially in an expensive city such as Toronto or Vancouver, is not easy.

That said, the horror stories she heard of never being able to afford another vacation or new pair of shoes hasn't become her reality. Instead, she's learned to save money and prioritize what she spends it on. "Because you have a nice place, your own kitchen, you stay at home and cook more. You find different priorities," Natalie says. "I get a real satisfaction knowing that it's my place, and even though I owe a bunch of money to the bank, it's my debt."

To ensure that you can still afford some fun in your life while paying a mortgage, financial expert Patricia Lovett-Reid recommends you don't buy more home than you need. If you are single, that means buying a four-bedroom home is likely too much. It's no surprise many single women turn to condos—they have enough space for one person, and they are affordable.

The flip side of buying only as much home as you need is buying only as much as you can comfortably afford. That also means not getting pressured into bidding wars if you cannot afford to go over the asking price. Many people wind up overextending themselves financially because they become emotionally attached to the place for sale. They picture themselves living there, and simply cannot let go. "Emotions can often be hazardous to your wealth," Patricia says.

"People treat their home differently than they treat their investment portfolio. They say 'I love this home. I will never find another one like it.' Yes, you will." Patricia's advice? "Don't fall in love with any of your investments."

So how do you know how much mortgage you can carry? As a starting point, you should follow the 32 percent gross debt ratio and 40 percent total debt ratio rules discussed in Chapter One. CMHC has also come up with some examples of housing affordability based on income levels shown in the table on the next page. All figures are based on a mortgage interest rate of 8 percent, the average tax and heating costs in Canada, and the mortgage an average Canadian would qualify for based on a 32 percent debt service ratio.

On a salary of $50,000 per year

- If you put down 5 percent ($7,500), you can afford a maximum of $150,000; if you put down 10 percent ($15,800), you can afford a maximum of $158,000; with 25 percent down ($47,400), you can afford a maximum of $189,600.

Income, Home Price, and Down Payment Guide

Household Income	5% Down Payment	Maximum Home Price	10% Down Payment	Maximum Home Price	25% Down Payment	Maximum Home Price
$25,000	$3,000	$60,000	$6,300	$63,000	$18,900	$75,600
$30,000	$3,900	$78,000	$8,200	$82,000	$24,700	$98,800
$35,000	$4,800	$96,000	$10,100	$101,000	$30,300	$121,200
$40,000	$5,700	$114,000	$12,000	$120,000	$36,000	$144,000
$45,000	$6,600	$132,000	$13,900	$139,000	$41,700	$166,800
$50,000	$7,500	$150,000	$15,800	$158,000	$47,400	$189,600
$60,000	$9,300	$186,000	$19,600	$196,000	$58,800	$235,200
$70,000	$11,050	$221,000	$23,400	$234,000	$70,100	$280,400
$80,000	$12,500	$250,000	$27,200	$272,000	$81,500	$326,000
$90,000	$14,400	$288,000	$31,000	$310,000	$92,800	$371,200
$100,000	$16,275	$325,500	$34,800	$348,000	$104,300	$417,200

Figures are rounded to the nearest $100.

All figures are based on a mortgage interest rate of 8 percent, the average tax and heating costs in Canada, and the mortgage on average Canadian would qualify for based on a 32 percent debt service ratio.

Source: Taken from the Canada Mortgage and Housing Corporation website (http://www.cmhc.ca).

On a salary of $70,000

- If you put down 5 percent ($11,050) you can afford a maximum of $221,000; with 10 percent down ($23,400), you can afford a maximum of $234,000; with 25 percent down ($70,100), you can afford a maximum of $280,000.

On a salary of $100,000

- If you put down 5 percent ($16,275), you can afford a maximum of $325,000; with 10 percent down ($34,800), you can afford a maximum of $348,000; with 25 percent down ($104,300), you can afford a maximum of $417,200.

As you can see, the more money you have up front, the more home you can afford to buy. Also remember that lower interest rates help make home ownership more affordable, which explains the popularity of home ownership in recent years, and in particular among single women who may have found it unaffordable when rates were higher.

Preapproval Reprise

Getting a good interest rate is one of the many negotiations you will go through in the home-buying process. As discussed in Chapter One, it's a good idea to get a preapproved mortgage before you go house hunting because it tells you how much home you can afford and will make your offer more attractive to sellers.

But the other big advantage to preapproval is that you can lock in an interest rate with your lender. Banks or brokers will usually guarantee the interest rate you negotiated during the preapproval process for about 30 to 120 days. This is a good idea in a rising interest-rate environment. If rates go down during this time, you can always renegotiate.

One you've got the mortgage terms and the interest rate nailed down with the lender, you can start looking. Once you find a property that you want to make a bid on, there is one more hurdle to clear in the preapproval process—the appraisal. The bank will want to assess the property's value for itself (remember the 5 C's of credit?). The appraisal establishes the market value of the property based on what it might reasonably sell for at that time in an open and competitive real estate market. The bank does this to ensure the home will sell for at least the amount of money they are lending you.

In my experience, the appraisal process was a breeze, and I didn't have to pay for it. For each of the three homes I purchased, the bank simply had an appraiser drive by the location (if that), and later do a market evaluation to ensure the price was consistent with the market conditions.

An appraisal can be a problem if you're making an offer that is well above the asking price, which usually happens in a bidding war. For example, if a home is listed at $275,000, but in a bidding war you offer to pay $325,000, the bank will determine if that is a competitive price, taking into considering market conditions. If you are only approved for the amount of $275,000, you will have to come up with the rest of the money on your own—or let that house go to another bidder.

Understanding Mortgages

You know that you'll be making a mortgage payment every month. Let's break down where that money will be going.

A mortgage is a contract between you and the bank that allows you to buy a property based on repayment terms. The mortgage principal is the amount of the loan you take out to buy the home. Let's say you plan to buy a home for $250,000. You have saved $50,000 for the down payment and need to borrow $200,000—that $200,000 is your principal.

You will then pay interest on that loan, which is the amount you will negotiate with your lender. Each time you pay that mortgage you are making an interest payment as well as paying down the principal.

A $200,000 loan at 5 percent will cost you about $10,000 in interest annually. If the interest rate is 6 percent, you will pay about $12,000 a year in interest. As you can see, the lower the interest rate, the more money you can put towards your principal.

The amortization period is the total length of time it will take for you to pay down your mortgage, and it's one factor used to calculate your monthly payments. The standard amortization period is 25 years, although even longer terms are now available. The longer your amortization period, the smaller your monthly mortgage fee will be. On the other hand, the shorter the amortization period, the faster you can pay off the mortgage, and the less interest you will be paying the lender in the long run.

The mortgage term is the length of time a lender will loan you the money for your home. Most mortgage terms run from six months to five years. After that time, you will either pay off the balance of the loan, or renegotiate it for another period of time. Banks often penalize you for breaking the mortgage term early—for instance, if you have a non-transferable mortgage and you sell the house before the term is up. That said, I have negotiated with my bank to reduce penalties and, for the last mortgage I had, to waive the full penalty for breaking the mortgage. I struck a deal saying I would invest the money I made off the sale into one of their banking products—which I had planned to do anyway. Remember Donald Trump, and "negotiate everything."

Your mortgage payments are calculated using the principal, the interest rate offered for the term, and the amortization period.

Let's look first at how the interest rate affects your total outlay of money over the life of the mortgage. I'll use the example of a $200,000 mortgage for a term of 5 years (60 months) at an interest rate of 6 percent over an amortization period of 25 years (300 months). This does not include mortgage insurance.

- Your monthly payment = $1,280

- Amount paid towards your principal over 5 years = $20,338

- Amount paid on interest over 5 years = $56,439

- Your balance at the end of 5 years = $179,662

- Total interest you will pay over 25 years = $183,772

- Total disclosure (all principal and interest payments) = $383,772

Now let's look at the same example, but with an interest rate of 5 percent:

- Your monthly payment = $1,163

- Amount paid towards your principal over 5 years = $22,993

- Amount paid on interest over 5 years = $46,799

- Your balance at the end of 5 years = $177,007

- Total interest you will pay over 25 years = $148,889

- Total disclosure = $348,889

As you can see, with the lower interest rate you will save $34,883 in interest over the life of the mortgage. (Calculator source: http://www.canadamortgage.com/calculators/amortschedule.cgi. You can calculate your own hypothetical mortgage terms using this link, or you can have your bank do these calculations for you.)

Now let's look at the impact of your down payment. Take, for example, a $250,000 mortgage, amortized over 25 years at an interest rate of 6 percent. How much interest would you pay if you put down 25 percent instead of 10 percent? Keep in mind that a 10 percent down payment is considered a high-ratio mortgage, which means you'll have the added cost of CMHC insurance for the mortgage.

- 25% of $250,000 = $62,500

- Your principal = $187,500

- Total interest paid over the life of the mortgage = $172,409.56

- Total disclosure = $359,909.56

10 percent down for the same mortgage agreement:

- 10% of $250,000 = $25,000

- Minus 2% ($4,500) for CMHC insurance plus GST ($270) = $20,230

- Your principal = $229,770

- Interest amount = $211,279.66

- Total disclosure amount = $441,049.66

Here is another way of looking at the savings:

- Monthly payment with 10% down = $1,470.18

- Monthly payment with 25% down = $1,199.72

- Monthly payment savings = $270.46

- Total difference over 300 payments (number of payments in 25-year mortgage) = $81,138

When you take into account the original difference in the down payments ($62,500 minus $20,230 = $42,270), you still have net savings of $38,868. (Source: TD Waterhouse Canada Inc.)

As you can see, the lower your interest rate, and the larger your down payment, the less you'll pay in interests over the years, and the more you can pay down on the principal of your mortgage. Your goal as a homeowner is to pay down that mortgage as quickly as possible.

The Home Buyer's Plan

You've seen how much money you can save by making a substantial down payment when you buy a home. But what if you don't have all that much socked away? One way to put more down is by making use of the federal government's Home Buyer's Plan (HBP).

Under this plan, first-time homebuyers can take out up to $20,000 from their Registered Retirement Savings Plan and put it towards buying or building a home. You can take out the money from your RRSP without paying tax, but have to pay back the funds within 15 years. Payments have to be made to the RRSP annually, starting the second calendar year after the year of withdrawal, until the money is paid back in full.

For instance, if you take out $20,000 from your RRSP in 2007, you will have to start paying it back in the 2009 tax year. The minimum annual payment from that point is one-fifteenth of the total you took out. So, if you took out the full $20,000, your payment would be $1,333.33 every year for 15 years. You can pay it back sooner, but if you miss a payment it will be included in your income for that year.

Some conditions to qualify for the HBP include:

- You must have a written offer-to-purchase agreement to buy or build a qualifying home. The agreement may be with a builder or contractor, or with a realtor or private seller.

- You plan for the home to be your principal place of residence.

- Your HBP balance on January 1 of the year of the withdrawal is zero.

- You are a Canadian resident.

- You buy or build the qualifying home before October 1 of the year after the year of withdrawal.

Other Down Payment Sources

Let's face it, while single women are more independent today than ever before, some of us, sometimes, need a little financial help. It's not uncommon for parents to pitch in for the down payment—and the same goes for men, and even for married couples.

Natalie says she got some help from her grandmother who was very proud of her for taking the leap into home ownership as a single gal. "My grandmother couldn't even vote when she was my age, and here she is helping her granddaughter buy her own place. She was thrilled for me," Natalie recalls.

If you do receive money from parents or grandparents, you will likely need a "gift letter" for your bank to show where that money is coming from, and to prove that the money is an outright gift, rather than a loan, with no strings attached. A loan—even a long-term, no-interest loan from your folks—will be seen by the bank as a second mortgage on the property, and will likely make it impossible for your bank mortgage to be approved.

Money is one thing, but some women may also need help getting the loan approved. The bank may wish to have another person guarantee the mortgage, which means that if you, the mortgagee, should default on payments, the guarantor agrees to make sure the payments are made. The guarantor can also be called a co-signer.

Esther, whom you met in Chapter Two, bought her first home by herself following a divorce. But she had to get her ex to co-sign on the mortgage. "It bothered me because I didn't have the credit rating I needed. The bank wouldn't give me the mortgage on my own, even though I had the down payment and a job." Luckily, she and her ex had parted as friends and he was happy to sign the necessary papers. It still left Esther wishing she could have made the purchase without his help.

Which Type of Mortgage Is Right for Me?

Conventional or High-Ratio?

There are two main types of mortgages, conventional and high-ratio.

A conventional mortgage means you've put down at least a 25 percent down payment on the home. For example, if the purchase price is $300,000, you will need to put down $75,000. Doing this exempts you from paying mortgage insurance.

A high-ratio mortgage means you have less than 25 percent of the total purchase price, and will need to get the mortgage insured. In Canada, the two major mortgage insurers are Canada Mortgage and Housing Corporation (CMHC) and Genworth Financial Canada. The insurance protects the bank if you default on the loan. The insurance premium varies between 0.5 and 2.9 percent, depending on the mortgage amount.

Fixed or Variable?

There is great debate among buyers on which mortgage is best: fixed or variable.

A fixed mortgage means your interest rate (and therefore your payments) are the same over the life of the loan. The interest rate on a variable mortgage fluctuates with overall interest rates, meaning your payments will vary. While studies have shown variable rates can be less expensive over time, many people choose a fixed rate because they want a set, predictable sum to pay each month.

Sheena, from earlier in this chapter, says she chose fixed because she wanted to pay a consistent monthly fee. "I don't look to see if the interest rate is going up or down. I have enough on my plate, and I'm not into that," she says. "I've budgeted, I have a lifestyle I want to maintain. I love to shop, so I need to stay on a budget. It's the first time I've been on a budget in my life!"

Open, Closed or Convertible?

It sounds more like the sunroof of that Mini Cooper you saw zooming down your street, but mortgages do come open, closed or convertible.

An open mortgage is one that you can pay off, renew or refinance at anytime without penalty. The catch is that you often pay a higher interest rate for this privilege.

A closed mortgage has a fixed interest rate and a set term that cannot be changed without penalty. The advantage is that you typically get a lower interest rate. Many closed mortgages allow you to make an annual prepayment of 10 to 20 percent. There are many variations of this, so ask a lot of questions about what you can and can't do.

A convertible mortgage is similar to a closed mortgage, but can be converted to a longer term without penalty. There are also mortgages that have a "conversion" feature that will allow an early renewal into a shorter length term. It's best to check with your lender on the options for this type of mortgage.

Zero Down Mortgage

You may also qualify for a "zero down mortgage" if you have a substantial income, a good credit rating and you plan to live in the home you are buying. In March 2004, CMHC relaxed its rules to allow borrowers to make down payments from any source, including borrowed funds and lender incentive programs. Prior to that, borrowers had to provide the down payment from their own pocket, or that of an immediate family member.

While this program is a great way to help people to become homeowners, it sends a chill up the spine of those who don't believe in carrying too much debt. Remember that the larger your mortgage, the larger the monthly payments. You will also wind up paying more interest to the bank over the long term.

These are some of the basic types of mortgages. As a buyer, you have many mortgage options and should choose the best one for you.

Our friend Jennifer chose a mortgage that allowed her to pay an extra annual payment of up to $10,000. Those payments are applied directly to the principal, rather than being eaten up by interest. That greatly reduces the amortization period of the mortgage. "At the time I negotiated that I thought, 'There is no way in hell I will have that kind of money sitting around to dump into a mortgage.' But now, I'm glad I have the option."

When you negotiate your mortgage, try to imagine your financial picture in the future. You will be surprised at how much of a saver you will become when you own a home. After all, you saved that money for the down payment and haven't started eating Kraft Dinner each night—at least not yet.

Now let's talk about other costs associated with buying your own home.

Other Expenses that Can Add Up

Many first-time homebuyers are surprised by the extra costs that crop up when you're finalizing the purchase of a home. It's best to set aside a few thousand dollars as "just in case cash."

Beth, our online editor from Newfoundland, says she was shocked by the many expenses apart from the down payment and monthly mortgage fees. "The big thing I wish I had known is that the down payment isn't the only expense up front. I was surprised by the different fees that came in—they hadn't even occurred to me." She hadn't budgeted for the other costs associated with home ownership, and ended up living off her bank overdraft for a few days.

Following is a list of up-front costs from CMHC to give you an idea of what other expenses may be involved in home buying.

✓ Mortgage loan insurance application fee and premium. If you don't put 25 percent down on your home, you'll need to pay for mortgage loan insurance. To get this insurance, you may be asked to pay the required application fee. Your lender may add the mortgage insurance premium to your mortgage or ask you to pay it in full upon closing.

✓ Appraisal fee. Your mortgage lender may require that the property be appraised at your expense. An appraisal is an estimate of the current market value of the home. The cost is usually between $250 and $350 and must be paid when you contract for those services.

✓ Deposit. This is part of your down payment and must be paid when you make an offer to purchase. The cost varies depending on the area, but it may be up to 5 percent of the purchase price. If you wish to make a down payment of 5 percent and you give a deposit of 5 percent, then your down payment is considered to be made.

✓ Down payment. At least 5 percent of the purchase price is usually required for a high-ratio mortgage and at least 25 percent of the purchase price is usually required for a conventional mortgage.

✓ Status certificate fee (not applicable in Quebec). This applies if you are buying a condominium (or strata unit, in British Columbia) and could cost up to $100.

✓ Home inspection fee. Remember that this may be a condition of your offer to purchase. A home inspection is a report on the structural and material condition of the home, and can cost between $200 and $400 (or more), depending on the complexities of the inspection.

✓ Land registration fees (sometimes called a land transfer tax, deed registration fee, tariff or property purchases tax). You may have to pay this provincial or municipal charge upon closing in some provinces. The cost is a percentage of the property's purchase price and may vary. Check with your lawyer/notary to see what the current rates are.

✓ Adjustments on prepaid property taxes and/or utility bills. If the vendor has prepaid the property taxes or any utility charges, your lawyer and the vendor's lawyer will work out how much you owe and the amount will be added to the amount owing on the day of purchase.

✓ Property insurance. The mortgage lender requires this because the home is security for the mortgage. Property insurance covers the cost of replacing the structure of your home and its contents. Property insurance must be in place by closing day.

✓ Survey or certificate of location. The mortgage lender may ask for an up-to-date survey or certificate of location prior to finalizing the mortgage loan. If the seller does not have one or does not agree to get one, you will have to pay for it yourself. It can cost in the $1,000 to $2,000 range. Buying title insurance may also be accepted by your lending institution in lieu of a survey. For complete peace of mind, you'll want both.

✓ Water quality inspection. If the home has a well, you will want to have the quality of the water tested to ensure that the water supply is adequate and the water is potable. Some municipalities offer water tests at no cost, but where payment is required you can negotiate these costs with the vendor and list them in your offer to purchase.

✓ Legal fees and disbursements. These must be paid upon closing and cost a minimum of $500 (plus GST/HST).Your lawyer/notary will also bill you the direct costs of checking on the legal status of your property.

✓ Title insurance. As mentioned above, your lender or lawyer/notary may suggest title insurance to cover loss caused by defects of title to the property.

(Source: www.chmc.ca)

I'll cover more of these closing costs in Chapter Six. In the meantime, remember to set aside some extra cash.

Even if you have all of your expenses in order, it's best to set aside funds in case of emergencies outside the home-buying process.

Helen, a forty-something hospital administrator, says she was aware of many of the up-front costs of buying a home, after doing it with her husband the first time. Then, when she bought on her own years after their divorce, Helen was caught off guard by some unplanned expenses.

A month after she moved into her newly purchased home in Pickering, Ontario, east of Toronto, her car broke down. In fact, it didn't just break down. It died. She had to buy a new one. The money she had set aside to buy new furniture for her first home as a single woman would have to go to buying a new car instead.

If that wasn't expensive enough, the water heater in her home broke down and she had to replace that too. "I laugh now and say my couch is the back seat of my car and the recliner is the front seat of the car and the stereo is my radio," says Helen with a healthy sense of humour.

Helen says she had heard all the horror stories about expenses and bad things that can happen to your home. "I thought, 'Well, what will be, will be. I will plan as best as I can'." But she adds that you cannot control life's surprises, and she still feels very positive about the experience. "They say that buying a house is one of the most stressful things in your life. I absolutely loved it. It was exciting, a new start. The fact that I was doing it on my own was very gratifying. I thought, if I can do this, I can do anything. I found it very empowering. It was an adventure."

Other expenses homeowners should consider when moving into a new home include:

✓ Appliances. Check to see what comes with the house, if anything.

✓ Gardening equipment.

✓ Snow-clearing equipment.

✓ Window treatments. Check to see what comes with the house.

✓ Decorating materials. Paint, wallpaper, flooring and tools for redecorating.

✓ Hand tools. You will need some basics, such as a hammer and a set of screwdrivers.

✓ Dehumidifier. May be required to control moisture levels, especially in older homes.

✓ Moving expenses.

✓ Renovations or repairs.

✓ Service hook-up fees for utilities. You may be required to pay a deposit for utilities such as telephone and heating services.

✓ Condominium Fees. You may have to make the initial payment for these monthly fees.

(Source: Canada Mortgage and Housing Corporation)

Insurance of All Kinds

I've talked about mortgage insurance, which you have to pay if you don't have a 25 percent down payment, but there are other types of insurance. You may want to consider mortgage insurance, and you'll be required to buy insurance for your home itself.

Mortgage Insurance

Your lender will likely try to sell you two types of insurance at the time you sign the mortgage papers: mortgage life insurance and mortgage critical illness insurance. Both are morbid topics to touch on, but should be discussed.

Having mortgage life insurance means that, if you die, your mortgage payments will be made by the insurance company. It's really up to you, and based on your personal circumstances, if you want to buy mortgage life insurance. It's most commonly used by couples because it ensures that, if one person dies, the other person will be able to go on living in the home, without mortgage payments to worry about. If you're buying without a spouse, you'll want to consider your beneficiary (or beneficiaries), and whether they want to take on your property, and your debt. Are you designating your parents or a sibling to inherit your house if you die? Having mortgage insurance gives them the option of keeping the house, or selling it for the full value it will have at the time of your death—either way, without payments to be made to a bank.

Mortgage critical illness insurance covers your mortgage payments if you become ill from certain serious illnesses such as cancer, heart attack or stroke. You can buy this separate from the mortgage life insurance. Especially if you're the only person living in the house and making payments on it, it can be a good idea to have this kind of insurance. Otherwise, you could find yourself extremely ill, unable to keep up with your mortgage payments—and forced to sell your house while going through a medical crisis.

Home Insurance

How you insure your property depends on whether you live in a house or a condo. Homeowners buy both property and contents insurance. In fact, most lenders will not give you a mortgage without proof you have purchased insurance on your property.

Condo owners, on the other hand, pay to insure their property through their monthly condo fees. This insurance covers only the items that are part of the building. What many condo owners don't realize is they need to buy separate insurance to cover their contents, which will include your personal belongings as well as any upgrades you have made to your unit. It's also recommended you have insurance for loss of use and personal liability insurance for injuries to visitors to your home or damage you accidentally cause to your neighbour's property.

Natalie, the Toronto condo owner, discovered the advantages of having homeowner insurance following a flood in her building in 2006. She woke up one day to the sound of running water down the hall from her unit. The flood, caused by contractors trying to repair the building's air conditioning system, damaged 21 units, including her own. While she managed to move her belongings out of the way before the water (with traces of glycol) reached her apartment, there was a lot of structural damage to some of her walls and floors. The repairs were covered by the building insurance she and others in the building pay through their monthly condo fees. But Natalie didn't have contents insurance. If she did, she could have stayed in a hotel during the renovation. Instead, she suffered through three months of contractors repairing and repainting her unit while working night shifts at a new job.

"I was forced to live in the disaster zone of noise, dust and chaos. My neighbour across the hall, who is single, nearing middle age and owns her own place, scolded me for not having insurance, since it is really only a couple hundred dollars a year!"

Natalie has since purchased insurance for the contents of her condo.

Now that you know all the do's and don'ts of finances and what surprise expenses to expect, you should feel confident about making your home-buying decision. In the next chapter I'll walk you through the offer process, including what conditions to include, for both new and resale homes and condos.

Checklist: Finances

✓ Save for a down payment.

✓ Establish a credit rating.

✓ Clean up any bad debt.

✓ Figure out how much you can afford to buy.

✓ Choose a bank or broker to negotiate mortgage/interest rate.

✓ Choose a mortgage that meets your needs.

✓ Budget for the various closing costs.

✓ Buy home and contents insurance.

✓ Consider mortgage life and mortgage critical illness insurance.

Common Mistakes to Avoid:

✗ Not cleaning up your credit.

✗ Buying more house than you can afford.

✗ Not negotiating the lowest interest rate possible.

✗ Not picking the mortgage suited to your needs.

✗ Forgetting to budget for extra fees upon closing.

✗ Forgetting to buy insurance.

5

Making the *Offer*

$\mathcal{I}$t was a warm May evening in 2002 when Jennifer went with her agent to make the offer on her downtown loft. When they arrived at the building, a four-storey former Gillette razor factory converted into 46 units, Jennifer realized she wasn't the only one interested in buying. She had just walked into a bidding war.

Her agent went in first to talk to the vendors and their realtor.

In the meantime, Jennifer waited outside on the sidewalk feeling the presence of competition just a few feet away. "When my agent came back, he said, 'You have to decide: Do you really want it?'"

Jennifer had just seconds to think. Did she really want the condo? If she did, she would have to offer a higher amount than the $209,000 asking price. Her mind was racing. Was this how she wanted to buy her first home?

Jennifer said yes. She instructed her agent to go in with an offer of $215,000 (her mortgage preapproval gave her the comfort to do so). He returned to the unit to present the offer to the sellers and their agent. Jennifer waited for what felt like hours. "I remember pacing around outside. In my mind, I was kind of hoping I wouldn't get it, and at the same time really wanting it," Jennifer recalls. "At that point, your fate is in the hands of someone else."

Minutes later, her agent walked up to her with the news. "I remember he said, 'You got it!' I wasn't feeling at all like 'Woo-hoo' excited. Instead, I remember feeling like, 'Wow, I've actually done it.'" Jennifer says she was a little freaked out for the next few hours and didn't sleep much that night, but the next day she knew it was the right decision for her.

Making an offer on a property is both an exciting and stressful step. The exciting part is that you've finally found that home you see yourself living in longer term. It's stressful because, once you've made that commitment on paper, there is no turning back.

A common misconception among first-time homebuyers is that the offer can be changed or even pulled. Here's the bottom-line: If the seller rejects the offer, makes a counter-offer, or doesn't respond to your offer, you still have options. You, the buyer, can either accept or reject the counter-offer. However, if you make an offer that the seller accepts, you have a legally binding contract (subject to any conditional clauses you may have added, such as approval for financing and a satisfactory home inspection report). You cannot back out from the deal. This is why it's very important to make sure that you want that home, and that your offer reflects all your conditions before you sign on the dotted line.

In this chapter I'll take you through the steps of making an offer for both a new and resale home. I'll also walk you through the conditions you should include in the offer of purchase and sale.

Before You Bid

I hate to nag, but before you go asking for that home you want, make sure you are preapproved for a mortgage. As mentioned in previous chapters, preapproval makes you a more attractive buyer, and means you haven't wasted people's time (including your own) if you find out you cannot get the loan.

Another thing to be sure of is that you want to live in that area. (Recall the qualities of a good location from Chapter Three.) As a single woman, you want a home that is not only safe, but one that suits your lifestyle.

Finally, know your financial limits.

Ruth, a divorcee and artist based in Hamilton, Ontario, says she stayed focussed on her price range when she moved from her condo in Toronto's Distillery District. "I knew what I wanted to spend, my maximum price. As a single person, it's not like you can turn to someone else and say, 'Oh, I cannot make the mortgage payment this month. Can you take care of it?' If you cannot do it, you cannot do it."

Because she was on a tight budget, Ruth didn't turn up her nose at homes that required some renovation. "I knew that I liked to fix stuff up. I can make a few sacrifices, but not to the point where it's all being done by outside contractors either." She ended up buying a cozy two-bedroom home on a quiet Hamilton street. It needed work, but the price was right. Because she knew the type of property she wanted, and could afford, Ruth says making the offer was "easy."

Put It in Writing

Once you've found the home you want to buy, making the offer means more than coming up with a price. Offers contain a lot of legal clauses and contingencies to protect both the buyer and seller. Some of the basic items you need to put in the offer include:

- The price you are willing to pay.
- Conditions you need met such as financing, home inspection, updated survey, etc.
- What you want included in the sale (for example, appliances, curtains and blinds, light fixtures).
- Amount of deposit.
- Closing date.

More on each of these below.

What Price Should You Offer?

You know what the seller is asking, but what price do you want to offer? How do you determine that number? Your agent will help you with this by looking at a few factors.

Recent Sales

First, your agent will look at recent sales of similar properties in the area. Realtors have access to the sale prices of homes through internal databases. It's another reason why having an agent working for you is a good idea. Knowing how much a similar home sold for helps you determine what price you should pay, and likely what price the seller is expecting.

Condition of the Home

Next, you and your agent will consider the condition of the home you want to buy when determining offer price. The structural condition of the property is important, such as a sound foundation, walls and ceiling that aren't cracked or show water damage, floors that don't resemble a Tilt-a-Whirl, and windows and doors that close. Roll a marble across a floor and see where it picks up speed. Don't hesitate to pull back curtains and move furniture to see what's behind it.

Carefully check the workmanship of any improvements that have been made to the home. Major improvements are also a factor when determining a home's value. For instance, newer kitchens and bathrooms and renovated basements are known to increase the market value of a home. Unless the property is blanketed by snow, you'll want to see how mature the landscaping is. If applicable, check out the condition of the garage and/or deck. Also, check with city hall to ensure there are no work orders outstanding on the property.

Market Conditions

Current market conditions also help determine price. If the market is hot, as it has been for the past several years in Canada, it's defined as a "seller's market." In this type of market, properties can sell fast. In a seller's market, the lucky seller can often expect to receive multiple offers, a practice that can drive homes to sell above the asking price.

It's a "buyer's market" when real estate sales are slow. Homes can sit on the market for many months and prices may even fall.

It's very tough to time the market. Your agent will look at the current market conditions to help you decide what price is best. Most real estate experts advise you to buy when the timing and conditions are right for you—that is, buy when you need to, not simply because you think it's a good time to get into the market.

Getting to Know the Seller

Finally, the agent considers how motivated the seller is to unload the property. The most common motivated seller is someone who is relocating to another area and has purchased a home in their new town or city. They want to sell quickly to avoid carrying two mortgages at once. Knowing a fact like this can give you an advantage when negotiating the price and other factors in the sale. Other reasons for selling may include family break-ups or other personal situations that force a sale of a property.

Toronto agent Darren Josephs says getting to know the seller can help you decide on how to structure the offer, including price and closing date. This doesn't mean inviting the seller over for dinner, or showing up at their door with a list of questions. Instead, Darren says your agent should be making the inquiries for you, either by talking directly to the seller, or to their representative.

The more information you have, the better your negotiating tools when it comes to drawing up the offer. "The number-one reason to get to know the seller is that their circumstances can affect the purchase price," says Darren. "If they are desperate to sell because of a divorce, or because they bought another house, it means they are going to be highly motivated to sell. That's good when it comes to negotiating price. If there is no urgency, they can sit on the price for a lot longer."

Another indication the seller may be eager to unload the property is when they keep dropping the price. Susan, a forty-something single woman in the advertising business, says the second condo she bought, in Toronto's moneyed Rosedale district, dropped in price three times before she decided to make an offer. It was February 1999, and the two-bedroom, two-bathroom, 1,000-square-foot space had been on the market for nearly five months. The seller had purchased the home 18 months earlier for $285,000. When it was first listed in the fall of 1998, it was listed at $319,000. The price was later cut to $299,000, and then cut again to $279,000.

Susan heard that the seller had recently moved out after inheriting some money, which explained why the space was empty. Susan saw this as an opportunity. "It was stale, overpriced, and had been on the market for too long," she recalls. The condo also needed some renovating, but Susan loved the space and saw the potential. Having some experience negotiating in her line of work, Susan says she was ready to put up a fight to get the property on her terms. What's more, when she was shown the property it was not very clean. She remembers seeing weeks' worth of dirty footprints on the hardwood floors, peeling wallpaper and a burnt-out light bulb in the main entrance.

"To me, that was worth a discount on its own." Susan got that condo for $260,000, including a 90-day closing date, which suited her personal circumstances at the time. "I figure I got the bargain of the century," she says looking back. The property value has nearly doubled since.

Hamilton realtor Angela Nolan says while an agent can go through all the factors to determine what price the buyer should offer, the decision is ultimately up to the seller. "It doesn't matter how much I, as an agent, and my client, decide the property is worth. It's really only worth what the seller is willing to let it go for." So if the vendor isn't going for your first offer, "either you'll have to decide to bite the bullet and pay a little bit more, or say the place isn't for you and move on."

Terms and Conditions of Sale

Price is arguably the most important part of the offer, but you might want to add some conditions to the offer. You should know, though, that having too many conditions can sour a sale, especially if you are in a bidding war for a property. In that case, the fewer conditions you attach to an offer, the better (more on this later). That said, some of the common conditions in an offer to purchase include:

- financing
- home inspection
- the sale of your current home
- legal review of purchase agreement
- updated land survey
- access visits

Financing

In a seller's market like the one we've seen in recent years across Canada, it's best to meet some of the conditions that apply to getting a mortgage before you make an offer. Having preapproval for a mortgage makes your offer more attractive to the seller.

Home Inspection

It's highly recommended that you pay an inspector to tell you about the condition of the property you are about to buy. An inspector can tell you if something is not working properly in the home, such as heating or plumbing systems, and if something needs to be upgraded (such as the wiring) or replaced (such as the roof). The home inspector will also point out repairs that will need to be done in the short and long term. The cost for this service is usually between $200 and $500, depending on the size and condition of the home. If you think you will be facing multiple offers on a home you want, you should have the home inspection done before making the offer. If there are expensive repairs that need to be made, you can walk away from the property or factor this cost into the offered price. Here is a list of components the home inspectors should be looking at:

- foundation
- doors and windows
- roof and exterior walls
- attic
- plumbing and electrical systems
- heating and air conditioning systems
- ceilings, walls and floors
- insulation
- ventilation
- septic tanks, wells or sewer lines
- any other buildings, such as a detached garage
- the lot, including drainage away from buildings, slopes and natural vegetation
- overall opinion of structural integrity of the buildings
- common areas (in the case of a condo)

(Source: Canada Mortgage and Housing Corporation)

While many condo owners skip the home inspection process, they shouldn't, because it's still a good idea, particularly in an older building. Inspectors have pointed out rotting decks, ceiling leaks and faulty appliances in condos that could have gone unnoticed.

If your condo is new and you don't want to hire an inspector, do your own thorough check of the unit. You should do this with your agent and/or a friend. Make sure the appliances work and the water pressure is good (turn on the shower, dishwasher and kitchen taps at once). Also check for any structural damage.

For more information on home inspections, I asked Jennifer Lucas, of AmeriSpec Home Inspection Service in Edmonton, a few questions.

1. *Why is it important to have a home inspector look at a property both before you buy and even before you do any major renovations?*

We live in a "buyer beware" world, and as inspectors it is our job to take the emotion out of home buying and give the buyer an accurate picture of what the condition of the house is before they make their final decision. A thorough inspection will look at all the major systems (for example: heating, plumbing, electrical, roof) and give the potential purchaser an indication if there are problems in those areas. We are like a general practitioner in medicine: We identify potential problems and identify the specialist they should contact to have the problem assessed in more depth, or fixed. (For example, we might suggest contacting a heating contractor or foundation specialist.) Likewise, if the homeowner wants to renovate, we can provide them with a list of deficiencies in the home, and prioritize issues for them.

2. *How are single women different? I would think that many of them are less experienced with "handyperson work." So is having a home inspector not just look at the house, but also explain its characteristics especially important for single women homebuyers?*

We find that most single women are not as familiar with the maintenance and repair aspects of home ownership. Therefore, they sometimes feel overwhelmed if they are purchasing an older home. About 80 percent of what an inspector is going to find when inspecting an older home are maintenance issues. A good home inspector will take the time to explain how to fix things, or where to go for help, so that the buyer can get the answers they need to maintain the home. If the buyer is a first-time home buyer, the time spent with the home inspector is invaluable. We can point out things like main shut-off valves for the plumbing, explain how to maintain a breaker box, how to extend the life of the furnace, water tank, etc.

3. *Many people don't have home inspectors look at condos. When is it a good idea to bring in a home inspector for a condo? What work do they do that's different?*

The only thing that is different about inspecting a condo is that we don't mount the roof. It is a good idea to have a condo inspected because if the inspector does find something wrong with a common area, then it allows the prospective buyer the time to go back to the condo association and ask: 1) when repairs are going to be made; and 2) if there is enough money in the reserve fund for future upgrades, repairs, etc. Surprisingly enough, many clients walk away from condo deals because of reserve fund issues.

4. *What are some of the common mistakes people make when hiring a home inspector? What do they overlook?*

The most common mistake is hiring an inspector based on price alone. The old adage that "you get what you pay for," applies. Currently there are no standards that identify what qualifies a person as a home inspector, which means anyone can hang a shingle and call themselves an inspector. As a result, there are people doing inspections with little to no inspection training. They may not be around a year later for their clients because they have gone out of business. People should be interviewing inspection companies and asking them questions: What kind of training do their inspectors have? Do they upgrade training? Do they have errors and omissions insurance? When I spoke earlier about pointing a client in the right direction for help—for example, a heating contractor—an inspection company should not be handing out business cards of third-party companies. It would be a conflict of interest. How do you know if you really have a heating problem if the inspector is telling you to call his brother the heating guy for a consultation?

Another common problem is that some homebuyers don't attend the inspection. People feel they are going to be in the way. This is not the case. A home purchase is usually the biggest investment a person makes and they should feel free to ask as many questions as necessary until they are comfortable with the decision they are making.

continued

5. Can you tell me any anecdotes of the types of problems home inspectors encounter in inspections? This may include new and/or used homes.

A lot of people, when they think of home inspections, assume that problems are only found in resale homes. This is not the case. We have found brand new homes with no insulation in the attic, and plumbing not being connected properly, causing leaks throughout the home. Houses are being constructed so quickly nowadays that contractors assume the next guy will pick up where they left off. This is not always the case. No house is problem free. How many people go into their attics on a regular basis?

Sometimes the current homeowners are not even aware of a problem until we complete our inspection. We have identified safety and health concerns that homeowners were not aware of and were grateful we caught, such as gas leaks and elevated levels of carbon monoxide.

Unfortunately, we also find problems that the homeowner was aware of, but failed to disclose. We once had a Jacuzzi tub leak so badly that we thought is was going to fall through the ceiling. The tub didn't leak unless you filled the water above the jets and turned the jets on. I guess the homeowner thought we wouldn't use that much water during our inspection and that the problem would go undetected. It cost them the deal.

AmeriSpec also suggests asking a potential home inspector the following questions:

- Do you follow industry standards?

- Are you willing to supply me with a sample report?

- Are you a full-time home inspection company?

- What other home services do you offer?

- May I attend the inspection?

- How much time will the inspection take?

- When will the report be ready?

- Do you perform repairs on items you inspect?

- What will I receive with the inspection report?

- What will be inspected?

- How much will the service cost?

- Do you provide an inspection agreement that defines the scope of the inspection?

A final note on basic home inspections. As Jennifer Lucas noted, because the profession does not have a requirement that inspectors take courses or pass any tests, anyone can pass themselves off as a home inspector. It's therefore a good idea to get references, as you did for your agent, broker and lawyer. Also, most good home inspectors belong to a provincial or industry association such as the Canadian Association of Property Inspectors, www.cahi.ca (or www.otpq.qc.ca in Quebec). Don't be afraid to ask.

There are a number of other inspections you can get before buying your home depending on where you live, and your level of concern about the home or your personal safety. Some of these inspections can be performed in conjunction with the home inspection. You should ask your home inspector if they are able to cover any of these services, but many require a specialized inspection:

Carbon Monoxide Testing

This "silent killer" may be an issue in homes using fossil fuels (oil and natural gas). Carbon monoxide can be detected only with an analyzer. A clear and working ventilation system minimizes the effects of the gas, so have your inspector check it. For additional protection, install a carbon monoxide detector.

Energy Assessment

One valuable—and money-saving—service offered by leading home inspection companies is an energy assessment. It determines major areas of energy use and waste while suggesting steps that could save you hundreds of dollars annually in utility bills. It also helps protect the environment.

Termite Inspection

Although a pest inspection is no guarantee that termites will not infest your home in the future, it will provide a "wood-destroying pest and dry rot" report on any existing threat. Beware of termite inspectors who are also exterminators and/or provide repairs.

Water Analysis

Nearly 70 percent of respondents in a recent poll indicated concern about the quality of their drinking water. Some home inspection companies now provide water quality analysis, but it is important that they use only certified laboratories. It is advisable to test for lead, bacteria (such as cryptosporidium), and—in some rural areas—nitrates and coleiforms. Most lenders require testing of water from private wells prior to advancing funds. In some jurisdictions this analysis is provided free of charge by the Health Department, though they may provide tests for only a limited number of potential contaminants.

Radon Testing

Radioactive gas, found in the soil in some parts of Canada, has become a major health concern for homebuyers. Make sure the inspector is familiar with established radon-testing protocols and uses only approved equipment.

Lead Paint Testing

High levels of lead paint can be found in some homes built prior to 1978. Lead paint can cause health and developmental problems for small children if the paint is deteriorated or if it is present in dust.

(Source: AmeriSpec Home Inspection Service http://www.amerispec.ca/)

Sale of Your Current Home

If you own a home and still have to sell it, you can put in a condition saying the agreement isn't final until your home is sold. However, be warned that sellers rarely agree to this condition, especially in hot markets.

When Helen, the hospital administrator you met in Chapter Four, bought her home in Pickering, Ontario, her agent suggested she drop this condition from her offer. Helen panicked. "I thought, 'Ohmigod, I could be the owner of two homes!'" Her agent calmed her fears by saying she was sure her current home, which was located down the highway in Ajax, would sell before the closing date. The worst-case scenario, Helen thought, was that she would have to drop the price.

Helen sold the home within weeks, even after her new puppy barked non-stop during showings and destroyed the bedroom carpet after the deal was done (she replaced the carpet).

Legal Review of Offer

Other conditions can include a review of the offer by a lawyer. Lawyers prefer it if you show them the offer before you present it, but this is not always possible, particularly in a bidding war. If you have an experienced agent, he or she has done hundreds of these agreements and should be able to steer you through without legal counsel.

That said, if you are buying a new house or condo from a sales office that represents the builder, it is highly recommended that you have a lawyer review the contract first. (More on new home buying later in this chapter.)

Updated Land Survey

It's also important to get an updated land survey. The survey shows the location of your property, the lines where it begins and ends, and any buildings on it, such as the house and the garage. It also tells you if the property violates any easements or rights-of-way. If there's a problem, you could be on the hook down the road if a neighbour complains or the city comes to investigate the lot. Also, many lenders won't approve a mortgage without this document, though some may accept title insurance instead of a survey.

Pre-sale Access to the Property

Another condition to throw in is the ability to visit the home you are buying once or twice before the closing date. This gives you time to measure room sizes if you plan to buy new window coverings or furniture. Also, a visit near the closing date allows you to check on the property to ensure nothing has been altered or damaged since the time you agreed to purchase it. Call it a peace-of-mind visit.

"I want everything, including the kitchen sink"

Many properties for sale tell you in the listing what's included, and what's not. You'll see the acronyms in the listings, such as "elfs" (electric light fixtures), "fag" (forced air gas), "gb&e" (gas burner and equipment), and "cac" (central air conditioning), to name a few. Sellers will sometimes throw in extras such as window coverings and islands in custom-made kitchens. These moveable personal possessions are also known as "chattels." While sellers don't mind giving up some items, asking for too much, such as furniture and artwork, can put them off.

A Toronto agent tells a remarkable story of a buyer who requested the speakers he saw attached to the seller's home-entertainment system. The seller rejected the request, but the request was made again.

It became a sticking point that dragged out the offer process for days. Finally, the seller caved in and gave up his $500 speakers with the home he sold for roughly $500,000.

When I sold my first home, the buyer insisted on keeping the wooden coat rack that I had recently installed in the front hallway. I had gone for months without a proper place to hang my coats, umbrellas and the dog leash and had spent $200 on this item from an antique store. I guess the buyer noticed how special it was too. Originally, I resisted giving up the coat rack, having already decided on the perfect place to put it in my new home. Eventually, though, after the buyer's agent made the third request for the coat rack, I gave in.

The Deposit

You want the seller to know you are serious about this offer and intend to bargain in good faith. There is nothing like money up front to make your point. This is where the deposit comes in. You want to put down enough to show you are interested in buying the home, but how do you know how much is enough? In a bidding war, some agents report having lost out to other bidders with much larger deposits.

While there is no rule on how much to put down, the standard is about 5 to 10 percent of the purchase price. Remember this money is part of your down payment, so you will likely already have it saved up. The deposit is normally held in trust by the seller's agent until the sale is complete.

If you back out of the offer after it has been accepted and the conditions removed, you will likely lose this deposit to the seller. As well, you may face legal action. This is why it's crucial that you are 100 percent sure you are ready to make the offer before you sign on the dotted line.

Closing Date

You've set the offer price, asked for some conditions, requested the stereo speakers (just kidding), and have the deposit. Now, there is one more item to carefully consider before presenting the offer to buy that home: "closing time." It takes more than simply picking the date when you want to be living in your new home. Timing is everything, as they say. Things to consider include your current living situation (for example, how much notice do you have to give the landlord before moving out?), how much stuff you have, moving dates and how the closing process is handled—your lawyer will need enough time to get all the paperwork in order.

If you are currently renting, and have to give 60 days' notice to your landlord, try a closing day of a week or two before you have to move out. This gives you time to move from your old house into your new one. You might also try moving early or mid-month, instead of at the end like everyone else. That also includes moving on a weekday instead of a weekend. Movers charge less for these off-peak times.

Another common mistake homebuyers make is setting the closing date for the same day as their moving date. The closing date is the day you get the keys, which often doesn't happen until late in the day because of legal matters, such as registering the property at the provincial land office. If you've hired movers to begin loading your stuff at 8 a.m., they could be sitting around for several hours at your new place while you wait to get the keys. I have heard of some circumstances where the movers had another job to go to and were forced to leave the furniture on the street outside the buyer's new residence.

Moving is stressful enough; don't make it harder than it has to be. Think ahead.

Buying a Resale Condo

Buying a resale condo is different from buying a home. When you buy a condo, you buy two things: your individual unit, plus a share in the condo corporation that owns and maintains the land and all of the common elements including elevators, foyer, parking, etc. Just as you would inspect a property you are buying, you need to inspect the work of the condo corporation. This is done by requesting a "status certificate" from the property management company as part of your offer. A lawyer will look through this document for you.

The status certificate states which expenses are the responsibility of the condo corporation, which are your responsibility, and which are shared between the two. It also lays out what the monthly condo fees will be when you buy, and any scheduled increases. Also key in this document is information on the condo corporation's reserve fund. Condo owners pay into this reserve monthly, and it should be large enough to pay for any repairs or upgrades that may arise.

The certificate also says if there are any existing circumstances that may require a future increase in common expenses, sometimes known as a "special assessment." A special assessment is a sum of money the condo owners of a building must pay to the condo corporation to pay for major repairs to the building that cannot be covered by the reserve fund.

A status certificate also shows if the condo corporation is involved in any lawsuits. It's information that may not deter you from buying the condo, but that you should be aware of up front before finalizing the sale.

Presenting the Offer

Now that you've covered all the bases in your offer, it's time to present it to the seller. Your agent will do this on your behalf. This is the part of the process where the agent gets to perform. The process will either be quick and painless, if the offer is immediately accepted, or it can turn into a long evening of back and forth negotiation.

No matter what the circumstance, realtor Brad Lamb recommends that buyers "keep their eye on the prize" during the offer process. "Don't get freaked out by the pressure. It all happens in one night, before midnight; that's the way it is. We purposely do that because people make decisions when they are under pressure. Don't be discouraged by it all; just relax—you are doing the right thing."

Offers and Counter-Offers

Beth in Newfoundland was a patient negotiator. The first home she bought was listed at a much higher price than she wanted to pay. It went on the market in February, but didn't sell. The sellers then dropped the price in May.

Beth recalls her agent saying to her, "Don't jump. These guys are hungry." The house was listed for about $20,000 more than she wanted to pay. Beth presented an offer for the amount she could pay. The seller came back with an offer at $10,000 less than the asking price. Beth counter-offered again. She agreed to the last price they came back with, on some conditions, including a house inspection. That inspection showed the house needed a new electrical panel. Beth asked for a rebate from her offer price, based on how much it would cost to fix the problem. In the end, she got that house for $17,000 less than its listing price. She was happy.

Counter-offers are common in home sales. Your original offer is the first step in the negotiation process. Remember, your goal is to get everything you want, while the seller's goal is to get everything he or she wants.

The transaction will usually go one of four ways:

1. You make the offer. Offer is accepted. You just bought yourself a new home!
2. You make the offer. Seller makes a counter-offer, asking for a higher price and/or different terms. You sign the offer back (once, or more times if necessary) and agree to some or all of the terms. The vendor accepts your counter-offer. You have a deal!
3. You make the offer. The seller counters. You reject the counter-offer and decide not to make a subsequent offer. The deal is off. You go back to house hunting. Maybe it wasn't meant to be.
4. It's a bidding war. You make the offer. The house is sold to a higher bidder. You move on. After all, there are other houses.

Buying a New Home or Condo from a Builder

The purchasing process is different when you buy a new house or condo. You buy the property from the developer, which either has a sales office or is represented by a real estate agent. Instead of you presenting them with an offer to purchase, they present you with a purchase agreement.

These documents have standard clauses, but vary quite a bit depending on the condo project, and can even vary from unit to unit in one building. It's for this reason that it's best to bring a real estate lawyer into the process to ensure there are no hidden clauses that can catch you (and your bank account) off guard.

Toronto-based real estate lawyer and columnist Bob Aaron says a good lawyer will point out the "dangerous clauses" or "gaping loopholes" he says are typical in builder agreements. A lawyer will go through this agreement looking for ways to save you, the buyer, money. The lawyer should also explain many of the complicated clauses thrown in that builders often don't bother to explain. Some developers will refer you to lawyers, but it's best to get an independent one referred to you by your agent, family or friends.

continued

Just as you chose an agent to look after your interests in buying a home, you want your lawyer to do the same.

Bob has written extensively on builder sales agreements in his *Toronto Star* column. Below is some of his advice on those agreements, which I appreciate being able to offer to you.

✓ Find out who pays the new-home warranty enrolment fee and how much it is. In most cases, the buyer gets stuck with the cost, even though the warranty program charges the fee to the builder.

✓ Some agreements contain small charges that the builder tries to pass on to buyers. Many builders will delete these on request, since they really don't belong in a purchase agreement. These charges can include $25 or more to negotiate each deposit cheque and $250 to negotiate changes to the offer.

✓ Most agreements also contain larger charges, which can run into the thousands of dollars. Although there is no stated upper limit to these, most builders will cap them on request. Larger charges can include new taxes or levies imposed by any level of government, and connection charges for water, hydro and gas service.

✓ Every builder offer contains a clause that statements made in the sales office are not part of the deal. So, if the sales agent makes an important promise, put it in writing in the agreement. Some sales offices hand out a separate list of estimated extras, but they are not binding unless they're added as a schedule to the offer.

✓ Some builder agreements do not contain detailed floor plans. If a floor plan containing measurements is not a schedule to the offer, don't sign the offer.

✓ The same advice also applies to the exterior design or elevation of a house. Although beautifully rendered sketches of the home design are always handed out in the sales office, they are rarely attached to the offer as a schedule. As a result, they do not form part of the contract and the builder is free to alter the final exterior design.

✓ Remember that the advertised square footage of a house or condominium is always an exterior measurement—around the outside bricks. Ask what the interior usable floor space is.

✓ Most offers allow the builder to change the house size. The Tarion warranty program (for Ontario homebuyers) has a guideline suggesting that any size reduction should not be greater than 2 percent, but it is not binding. Make sure your agreement contains a clause guaranteeing the minimum house size to be delivered.

✓ In the same vein, most offers allow the builder to alter the interior house layout without the buyer's consent or knowledge. Buyers should discuss with their lawyers what happens if the house built is not the house they were expecting. I recommend this clause be deleted.

✓ Consider adding a clause to the offer guaranteeing a minimum lot frontage and depth. When it is registered, the plan of subdivision shows the lot sizes. As many agreements allow the builder to change the lot size without compensation, offers should require delivery to the buyer of a copy of the subdivision plan prior to the start of construction, to allow the buyer to verify lot size in advance.

✓ Insist on being provided with a copy of the architect's plans on closing. This will make later renovations or additions much easier.

✓ A recent wrinkle is for the buyer to have to rent the furnace and air conditioner. A monthly furnace rental can cost $75 or more—adding significantly to the carrying charges on a home. The offer should state if the furnace is a rental, and if so, how much the rent is.

✓ An increasing number of buyers believe in the ancient principles of feng shui: living in harmony with the energy of the surrounding environment. If this is an important factor, discuss with the builder whether these principles can become part of the house design.

continued

✓ Buyers may be concerned about whether there will be a hydro transformer, fire hydrant, street light or community mailbox in front of the house. If this is an important factor, it should be clarified with a specific clause in the offer.

✓ If the purchase price includes an extra charge for a premium lot, it should be clearly set out in the offer what features the premium lot will have—such as a larger size, better location or view, or proximity to a golf course, park or ravine.

✓ Occasionally, a builder will refuse to connect the appliances. Make sure the offer requires the builder to install and connect all appliances.

✓ When a sale closes, some of the purchaser's money will be diverted to pay off and discharge the construction financing.

✓ All purchase agreements contain a clause requiring the purchaser to accept a promise or undertaking to register a discharge of the builder's construction mortgages after closing. Unfortunately, many builder offers require the purchaser to accept a discharge undertaking given by the vendor and not its lawyer. If the builder is unable to discharge the mortgage, the undertaking may not be enforceable and the purchaser does not get clear title. When I review offers, I make it clear the undertaking must come from the lawyer, not the builder—this is not negotiable. If the offer has a builder undertaking only, I tell my clients I will not be able to certify clear title if the clause can't be amended.

✓ Licensed real estate agents are covered by errors and omissions insurance, strict codes of conduct, and extensive educational requirements, both before and after registration. Ask your builder sales rep whether he or she is a licensed sales agent.

✓ Ensure the offer requires the builder to complete any extras and upgrades that were ordered. Read the small print on the extras page—more often than not the tiny lettering allows the builder to omit the extra or upgrade and refund the extra cost. Many builders attach a schedule to the purchase agreement titled "Request for Upgrades." If an offer contains this type of schedule, the builder has the option not to supply the upgrades or extras. Extras or upgrades should be contractually binding, and not a mere request.

✓ Consider the builder's ability to extend closing. For a house, it can be 250 days from the closing date in the offer, and for a condominium, occupancy extensions can often run to two years. If you're selling an existing house, make sure you try to coordinate the closings so you do not wind up with two houses or none at the closing time.

✓ Virtually all builder offers prohibit the purchasers from visiting the home under construction due to insurance reasons. Frankly, I don't buy that argument. Insist on a contract clause allowing two or three visits before the house is finished.

(Source: Bob Aaron, *Toronto Star* column, April 2, 2005. Used by permission.)

If you are buying a new house or condo, you should also be familiar with the New Home Warranty Program in your province. This is a type of insurance that protects you, the buyer, if the developer cannot follow through with your deal. It also covers you if the developer is not around to fix any potential problems in your home after you move in.

The warranty period usually lasts one year after the closing date, but check your agreement for details. Also, be aware that you may not be moving in on the date they promise. Delays are as common for new homes and condos today as rising gas prices in the summer months. Expect it, and plan for it. (More on delays in Chapter Six.)

Assuming you got everything (or enough) of what you wanted when offering to buy that new home, and the seller agrees, you have a deal. The agreement isn't final, though, until you've both signed the papers. Once that's done—congratulations! You are a homeowner.

What's more, you are a single woman homeowner who was not afraid to do it on her own, and on your terms. Pat yourself on the back for surviving some of the most stressful stages of home buying. Your next goal is to make that space your home, sweet home.

In the next chapter I'll tell you how to get started. I'll also tell you what to expect between closing the deal and closing day.

Checklist: Before You Make the Offer

✓ Know your financial limits.

✓ Get preapproved for a mortgage.

✓ Figure out what price you're willing and able to pay.

✓ Set conditions such as financing, home inspection, updated survey, legal review.

✓ Know what's included in the sale such as appliances, carpets, electric light fixtures.

✓ Ask for items you might want included that aren't specified such as window coverings and light fixtures.

✓ Determine deposit amount.

✓ Decide on a closing date.

✓ Get a lawyer to review the offer, especially for a new house or condo.

✓ Be prepared for the offer to be accepted or rejected.

Common Mistakes to Avoid:

✗ Making an offer on a home that is more than you can afford. Stay within your price range. Being house poor is no fun.

✗ Not getting preapproved, especially when you may have to enter a multiple-bid situation. You don't want to lose a house simply because you kept putting off that appointment with the lender.

✗ Assuming the seller's agent will get you the best deal. Remember, they are acting for the seller. Get your own agent.

✗ Forgetting to include conditions where possible. Think closing dates, walk-throughs, home inspections, etc., before sealing the deal.

✗ Picking the wrong closing date. Think carefully about when you will move out of your current home. Don't rush the move if you don't have to. Take your time.

✗ Not consulting a lawyer to review your offer, especially in the case of buying from a builder's plan. A lawyer is trained to spot the "tricks" in any real estate transaction.

✗ Not taking a final walk-through before closing. You want to ensure the property is in the same condition as it was when you made the offer.

6

They Said Yes!
Now What?

Buyer's remorse. You've heard about it. You've probably even had it before. Remember those $500 shoes you just had to have, then wore once? How about that $2,500 tropical vacation package you bought, not realizing it was during rainy season?

Well, that house you just purchased was a little more expensive. I hate to start you off as an official homeowner on such a negative note, but buyer's remorse is common. So let's talk about it, and about how to get past it.

Just to prove how common it is, Wikipedia.org, the hugely popular online encyclopedia, has a substantial entry on buyer's remorse:

> *"Buyer's remorse is an emotional condition whereby a person feels remorse or regret after the purchase of an item. It is frequently associated with the purchase of high value items such as property, cars, etc. The common condition is brought on by an internal sense of doubt that the correct decision has been made. With high value items such as a property, this is exacerbated by the fear that one may have acted without full and complete information. … An equally common source of disquiet is a sense that one cannot actually afford the item."*

Had enough yet? Well, there's a little more, but this part should make you feel a bit better:

> *"Fundamentally, it is a natural human reaction, rising out of a sense of caution. It cannot therefore be considered 'bad' although it may also stem from a sense of not wishing to be 'wrong.' In an extreme situation, an individual who struggles with or cannot accept the possibility that they may have made a mistake, may be suffering from a more serious and severe condition that has truly little to do with 'buyer's remorse'. … Buyer's remorse, when evidence exists that it is justified, is a classical example of cognitive dissonance. One will either seek to discount the new evidence, or truly regret and try to renounce the purchase."*

Translation: It's all in your head.

Yes, buying a house is a big decision. In fact, it's likely the biggest financial commitment you will ever make. That being the case, you have a right to feel anxious. But no, you cannot cancel the contract now. That's the bad news.

The good news is this feeling will pass. Remember how much you wanted that house in the first place? The "high" you got when you found it? Also remember that you thought through this decision carefully. You hired the right professionals, you took the advice in this

book, and of those around you. Most importantly, you made this decision for yourself, and on your own. You aren't sitting at home in some
rented dump waiting for the right man to lead you towards the house
with the white picket fence.

Dealing with Buyer's Remorse

Still feeling queasy? Here are some practical "do's and don'ts" to help
you get beyond buyer's remorse.

Do:

✓ Make a list of the pros and cons of home ownership, and your wants and needs in a
home. You likely did this when you started house hunting. Go back and find that list.
Read it again. The good should outweigh the bad. Remember, you bought this house for
a reason(s).

✓ Think like a guy. Forget your feelings. Think practical. This house is good. Remember
those other houses you saw? You wouldn't be caught dead in those. You picked the
right one. Maybe it's just your time of month, which explains the anxiety? (This is a guy
talking, remember.)

✓ Talk to your agent. Remember your agent is not just your house finder and negotiator,
but also your counsellor. Call the agent and tell them you are feeling anxious. Agents
are trained to deal with this reaction

✓ Be prepared for this reaction. Just like you would have Kleenex ready for a chick flick, be
prepared for the emotions that may well up after you buy a home. Get a sample purchase
agreement before you buy. Take it for a test drive. Sign the document. How does it feel?

✓ Pay your purchase a visit. If you were wise, you put a clause in your purchase agreement
to drop by and see the home once or twice before the closing date. Take advantage of
this term sooner rather than later. Often, going to see your new home before you move
in helps ease the anxiety.

Don't:

✗ Don't keep looking at other houses. You've made a commitment. Stick with it. The grass isn't greener. Your grass is fine the way it is. Be happy with your decision.

✗ Don't ask others if you "did the right thing." While friends and family mean well, they don't always know why you chose the home you did. Remember, they weren't with you for the house-hunting experience. What's more, it's your decision. If it's your parents and they live in another area, they likely don't understand the market. My parents live in the country and nearly dropped dead when I told them what I paid for my little home in Toronto.

✗ Don't doubt yourself. Save the regret for the triple chocolate cheesecake you ate last night. That was a moment of weakness. Your home was not purchased on impulse.

✗ Don't try to back out. The consequences of backing out of your home purchase will cost you dearly. It's a legally binding contract now and trying to get out of it will mean losing your deposit, and potentially a long lawsuit. Stick with your decision.

Toronto realtor Brad Lamb says buyer's remorse is common. His advice: "Relax." But he acknowledges how difficult that is. "You would be a psychopath if you didn't feel the pressure that you are feeling. It's natural, but you cannot succumb to it. Every single person, when you are spending that kind of money, should feel pressure. Even if you made a mistake, you are probably going to stay for five years. Five years fixes any mistake you make in real estate. If you overpaid by $10,000, you'll forget about it in five years."

What if I Lose My Job?

Another common fear that comes with buyer's remorse is: "What if I lose my job?" You'll survive. I did.

I bought my first house in the summer of 2001. Remember, the row house with the rowdy neighbours? Well, less than three weeks before the closing date I was laid off. I was one of 130 people let go in a company "restructuring." I wasn't terribly upset about losing that job in particular, but losing the income just weeks before I was about to move into my first home was definitely a concern.

Shortly after I was fired, a couple of job offers came from different parts of the country. Did I want to move to Calgary? How does Ottawa sound? "I just bought a house," I would reply, as if my feet were stuck in cement blocks.

The truth is, I wanted that house. I had put down the money and I was not about to abandon it for something trivial like losing my income. I'm kidding, of course. I wasn't ready yet to leave the city, but I did start scrambling for freelance work the day after my job ended. Luckily, I had a severance package to carry me for a few months, and a friend lined up to be my roommate for a year while she saved to buy her own first home.

Losing your job can happen after you buy your home, but you survive it. You do it because you want to, and because you have to. If you were renting and lost your job, you would still have to pay the rent, wouldn't you? I guess you could move back in with your parents, but nobody wants that—including your parents.

Remember that buyer's remorse is just a feeling. You bought the home and you cannot go back. Instead of feeling anxious, look ahead. Owning your own home is an achievement. It's also a good investment in the long run.

Before You Get the Keys

There are still a lot of things to take care of before you get the keys to your new home. You need to work with your lawyer on the details of closing the home sale. Also, if you are renting, you need to tell your landlord you are moving out, or find someone to sublet.

If you own a home, you have to sell it. There's also moving day. What day should you move, and what's the least stressful way to get it done? Let's go through all of these below.

Love Your Lawyer

There are a lot of jokes about lawyers, but when it comes to buying a home, all kidding aside, you have to love your lawyer. First of all, you really cannot buy or sell a home without one. Second, if you used a lawyer before you signed the offer, he or she may have saved you money and future headaches by pointing out any tricks in the offer to purchase. Finally, your lawyer will deal directly with the bank, the seller's lawyer and your agent when it comes to wrapping up that deal. You have to respect a lawyer for taking care of all that for you.

Of course you pay for it, but remember, the closing costs aren't all fees you pay the lawyer. He or she is just the lucky person who has to collect all those fees.

What Does a Lawyer Do Here?

Now that you've come to an agreement to buy a home, your lawyer will oversee the process of transferring the property to you. Here's a list of what they do to earn what you pay them:

✓ Help you understand the sale agreement and how you will take on the deed.

✓ Check that there are no liens, covenants or easements on the property that could interfere with your purchase or use of it. A lien is a claim to property for the satisfaction of a debt; a covenant is a legal assurance or promise set out in a deed; and a property easement is a right to use some part of a property for a specific purpose (e.g., adjacent property owners may enter into an agreement to share a common driveway).

✓ Prepare and register all legal documents.

✓ Clarify your mortgage terms with you and talk to your bank about getting the money from your mortgage to the seller.

✓ Figure out how much money you owe the seller, including "adjustments" on taxes owing and utility costs paid before the closing date.

✓ Arrange title insurance, which protects you from losses as a result of any defects on the title. (Many lending institutions will accept title insurance in lieu of a survey. Even if you have a survey, however, title insurance is highly recommended.)

✓ Verify your home insurance is in place.

✓ Check the history of the property to make sure the seller actually does own it. This is also known as a "title search."

✓ Work with seller's lawyer to transfer the deed from the seller to you on the closing date.

✓ Get the keys from the seller, and hand them over to you on the closing day.

How Much Does All This Cost?

Legal fees are higher for a buyer than a seller. That's because a buyer's lawyer has more work to do (see list above). The fees you pay at the lawyer's office upon closing include:

✓ Lawyer fee and disbursements. This usually ranges from $800 to $1200. About $200 to $600 is the lawyer fee for the work. The total also includes about $200 to $600 for the title search and administration fees, including courier, fax and photocopies.

✓ Adjustments/settlement. Your lawyer will prepare a closing statement that adjusts and prorates all the required credits and charges associated with the property sale, such as taxes and utilities.

✓ Land transfer taxes. These are provincial taxes you pay when you buy property. The tax is calculated as a percentage of the purchase price and the formula varies by province.

✓ GST. You pay this if you bought a new home, or one that was completely renovated. This means you will also pay GST for the lawyer's service. Depending on the price of your home, you may be eligible for a GST rebate.

Those are the costs you pay at the lawyer's office. So, how do they add up in dollar terms? Let's say you bought a $300,000 home in Ontario. Here is an estimate:

Purchase price:	$300,000
Legal fee:	$1,000
GST (if applicable):	$69.93
Gov't registration costs:	$141.40
Title insurance:	$170
Land transfer tax:	$2,975
Total:	**$4,356.33**

Some lawyers charge a flat fee for their services. Others bill hourly. Either way, get an estimate up front of what your costs might be.

You should also plan to meet with your lawyer a day or two before the closing date. This gives you time to review the documents. The lawyer has a lot of other things to do on the closing date itself to handle your transaction, including getting your keys.

Bye, Bye Landlord

If you are renting, you need to tell your landlord you are moving out. Check with your provincial landlord-tenant legislation, but most should let you out of a lease with 60 days' written notice.

If for some reason you have to sublet to someone else until the term is up, be sure to choose a reliable tenant. If a subletter damages the place, or doesn't pay the rent, you, as the official tenant, are usually responsible. I'll go into more depth about being a landlord, from the perspective of a homeowner, in Chapter Nine.

Selling Your Home

If you own a home already, hopefully you asked for a long closing date to give you time to sell your current residence. If not, don't panic.

Get organized and get that home on the market ASAP. There are too many steps to selling your home to mention here, but go to Chapter Ten on selling your home and find out the best ways to get it done, quick! If you don't sell your home before you take possession of the new one, many banks offer "bridge financing," which allows you to carry two mortgages at once. Obviously, this is expensive, so selling your home first is best.

Moving In and Out

Before we talk about moving day, there are some little items to take care of when moving into your new home.

If your lawyer hasn't already done so, you need to contact the utility companies (electricity, water and gas) to have the meters read on the day your new home sale closes. The companies will then set up new accounts in your name. You should do this as soon as possible, but it's also a good idea to double-check a few days before the closing that this has been looked after.

You will need to contact the telephone and cable companies on your own to set up service. Do this as soon as possible, especially since it can sometimes take weeks to connect these services. Also, don't forget to disconnect these services at your existing residence.

Some companies will transfer the service for free. Don't forget to ask about this as a possibility.

Arrange for your move far in advance. Get quotes from at least three moving companies. Also, get references. Sometimes the cheapest moving companies aren't the best. Remember, these people are handling all your personal belongings, so hire a company you feel you can trust.

Finally, send out change of address notifications. This includes your family and friends, as well as the bank, your investment companies and government departments such as Canada Revenue Agency and the agencies that handle your driver's licence and health card.

Don't Book the Mover Just Yet...

If you bought a new house or condo you may wish to hold off on booking the mover and filling out those change of address forms. It's common for new housing projects to be delayed for months, sometimes even years. Unfortunately, this is allowed and your lawyer should discuss with you what your agreement says about delays.

In most provinces, there is no minimum notice period for delays. If the house isn't ready on the final closing day, a builder has the right to ask for a written extension without giving any notice. The purchaser's only options then are either to back out of the deal or agree to an extension. Many buyers are reluctant to back out of a deal, especially after having already waited months, or even years.

Many lawyers recommend that buyers negotiate extension provisions at the time the agreement is signed, and not during construction. A clause can be inserted into the original agreement of purchase and sale that requests the builder financially compensate the buyer for any delays. This type of clause doesn't always get accepted, but it's worth a try.

Occupancy Fees

Another, often annoying, part about buying from a builder's plan is that your move-in date is not necessarily the possession date. You may have the keys to your home, but it's not officially (legally) your place yet. If this happens, you have to pay an "occupancy fee" until the closing date.

Let's break it down by definition.

Interim occupancy: The occupancy of a proposed unit before you receive title to your home. In other words, you have the keys and you may even have already moved in, but the place is not officially yours yet. This is because the closing date has not yet happened. Until then, you normally pay the builder an occupancy fee.

Occupancy fee: Remember those rent cheques you paid your old landlord? Well, this scenario is not much different. In this case, the builder is your landlord. The occupancy fee is based on the following: 1) estimated monthly maintenance fee 2) estimated monthly realty tax and 3) estimated monthly interest.

Possession date: Also known as "closing date." This is when you officially take possession. The deed to this property is now under your name and you no longer have to pay the builder the occupancy fee. Now, you just pay the mortgage, the taxes and the maintenance fees, plus all other related expenses.

Sneak Peek Before Closing

Just before the closing date you should have scheduled a final inspection of the house you are about to move into. You should bring your agent, and even a few friends if you want. This pre-closing walk-through (also called a preinspection) is done to verify that everything you asked for in the purchase agreement is there. You don't want to find out after you move in that the dining room chandelier you loved—which came in the agreement—has been replaced by a cheap light fixture.

Walk-through for Resale Homes

When you do the walk-through for a resale home, pay attention to the attic, basement and garage. If it looks like there is a lot of junk lying around that may not be moved, tell your agent. The last thing you want is the previous owner's junk.

The day I moved into my first home, the previous owner was still moving out. His stuff was going out the back door, while mine was coming in through the front. When he finally cleared out at 1 a.m. he not only left behind cupboards full of dishes, pots and pans and Tupperware, but a pile of paint cans, hardware, boxes of nails and his former wife's wedding dress.

Even worse, he left behind one of his two cats, which I recognized from my previous visits to the home. On that first night, I heard loud, almost screaming cat cries from the backyard. When I went outside to investigate, I realized it was the cat, wanting to come into his house. Because I had two dogs at the time—mine, and my roommate's dog—the cat wouldn't have survived very long in his former space. I called the former owner, who suggested I find the cat a new home—in other words, not his. A few days later, after sending out a few emails to friends, I managed to find a good home for the cat. I later returned the wedding dress to the owner, along with boxes of the junk he had left behind. It wasn't the kind of happy new home experience I was expecting.

Back to the walk-through. Here are some tips for reviewing your soon-to-be new home:

✓ Check your emotions at the door. Swoon over the space another time. This inspection is serious and to ensure everything is how it should be as stated in your purchase agreement.

✓ Don't miss a room. Check the house from top to bottom, including closets and laundry rooms, etc.

✓ Pay attention to the expensive parts of the home you get to keep, and the items you were most attracted to, such as light fixtures, window coverings, etc.

✓ Look closely at areas where rugs or furniture were when you first saw the home. Defects in carpet or floors may now be visible and should be noted.

✓ If an item is missing that should be there, mention it now. You want it handled before closing, or it could be too late.

Walk-through for New Homes

Your walk-through for a new home or condo is a bit different. Plan to be a lot more picky. If you see any problems, you need to point them out to the builder to have them fixed before you move in, or shortly after. Remember, new homes in most cities are covered by a warranty. Double-check the rules in your area.

When I bought my loft in Toronto, the walk-through uncovered a number of things that needed to be repaired. The bathtub was not properly sealed and the tap in the tub was too short, meaning the water spilled out around the edge instead of landing directly in the tub. Some of the lights didn't work, the smoke detector didn't have a battery and there was a large crack in the kitchen's granite countertop. I made a list of the problems and the builder had them fixed within a few weeks.

Sheena, the business development manager you heard from previously, brought five friends with her for the walk-through. Together, they scoured the 992-square foot space looking for any defect, large or small. "I knew I was going to find things wrong simply because they [the builder] made it sound like they were going to scramble to get it done on time," Sheena says.

The results? The paint job was so poor there were still droplets on the stairwell and around some of the doors, Sheena recalls. What's more, there was plaster stuck to the cement floors and the cupboards were installed incorrectly. Sheena and her team even discovered that the roll where the toilet paper was to hang had not been installed.

"I think the developer wanted to kill me," she says of her pre-closing inspection. "We went over that place with a fine-tooth comb." She recalls one of the executives from the development company rolling his eyes after she pointed out some of the defects in her condo. "I caught him doing it and called him on it front of everyone." Nobody talked down to her after that, and the work was done.

Sheena's advice to other single women dealing with developers: "Don't let them push you around. They try to hurry you along [in the walk-through]. People should take all the time they want to look everywhere and test everything out."

It should be said that builders are not necessarily out to get you. Just like you make mistakes on the job sometimes, so do builders. This doesn't mean you should excuse them, but instead, point out the errors and get them fixed.

The Canadian Home Builders' Association (CHBA) says the preinspection not only helps you see if everything has been built properly, but allows the builder to familiarize you with the systems and products in the home, and how to operate, maintain and service them.

Your builder will use an inspection sheet that you will be asked to sign at the end of the inspection. Write down everything that you think requires attention or correcting on that sheet. This includes minor imperfections. This is done so that there is no argument later about who is responsible for the item that needs to be fixed.

Here is a list of some of the items the CHBA recommends you look at closely during the walk-through.

Outside

✓ Siding: should be even, level and clean, with no awkward seams, no nails showing

✓ Brick exteriors: no gaps in the mortar between bricks; weep holes intact

✓ Windows and doors: verify placement, colour and styling details

✓ Caulking: check around windows, doors and electrical outlets for even application

✓ Paint and stains: look for even coverage and proper colour

✓ Shutters, trim and other decorative elements: verify colour, styling details and secure installation

✓ Fascia, soffits, eavestroughs, downspouts: check for proper colour and secure installation

✓ Roofing: verify material, colour, style; also duration of manufacturer's warranty

✓ Stairs, railings: check styling details, colours, solid installation

✓ Lights, electrical outlets and doorbells: check placement and test that they work

✓ Garage doors: should open and close easily; door to the house must be self-closing

✓ Grading around the house: should slope away from the foundation to divert moisture

✓ Driveway, walkways, sodding and other landscaping: Has work been done according to specifications? If weather prohibits completion now, when will it be done?

Inside

✓ Walls and trim: confirm colour; check for even paint coverage, no visible seams, no nail pops, no nicks and scratches, smooth grouting between wall tiles

✓ Flooring: verify selection and installation, colour and grade; minimum of squeaks and spring; no ragged seams or edges and no gaps or scratches; even grouting between tiles

✓ Windows: should open and close easily, have proper screens and no cracked panes

continued

✓ Doors: must be well-fitted and properly hung for easy opening and closing; check glass or mirror panes for cracks or nicks; test locks on outside doors

✓ Cabinets, drawers, closets: check for smooth operation; proper configuration of shelving and dividers; confirm handles and knobs

✓ Countertops: no nicks, scratches or uneven seams

✓ Faucets: turn off and on to verify smooth operation; no leakage or drips

✓ Plumbing fixtures: check for chips or scratches; look for caulking around all fixtures; run water to verify good drainage; flush toilets

✓ Electrical, cable and other outlets: verify placement and test if they are live

✓ Light fixtures: turn on and off to see if they work

✓ Basement: no cracks in the walls or signs of leakage; a floor drain in the lowest part

✓ Upgrades and options: refer to the contract to make sure nothing has been overlooked

You should also be sure to get a demonstration of any products in the home, such as appliances, security systems and furnace and central air systems. You should be given manuals for these items and they should include manufacturer's warranty and maintenance information. Your builder should also give you information on warranties by subcontractors for products and services that went into the construction of your home.

(Source: Canadian Home Builders' Association)

Closing Day

This is it. This is the day you've been working towards for many months. Closing day is when the deed is transferred to you. You are now the legal owner of this space you've been dreaming about.

Well, almost. There are a few more steps required.

✓ Your lender gives your lawyer the mortgage money.

✓ You give the balance of the purchase price to the lawyer, along with the closing costs.

✓ Your lawyer/notary pays the seller and registers the home in your name.

✓ Your lawyer provides you with a deed.

And, finally, you get the keys! Congratulations, again.

Now that you are officially in your new house, you will want to make it feel like home. This may mean renovations, a fresh paint job, or buying new furniture. In the next chapter I'll talk about all of the above, and just how much it could cost. Just when you thought you'd spent enough money...

Checklist: Now that You've Bought

✓ Be prepared for buyer's remorse.

✓ Hire a lawyer to handle closing details.

✓ Set aside enough cash for closing day, moving, etc.

✓ Pick a closing day that gives you time to move.

✓ Schedule one or two walk-throughs before the closing date.

Common Mistakes to Avoid:

✗ Letting buyer's remorse get you down.

✗ Not setting aside enough time to move from one home to another.

✗ Not saving enough money to pay for legal fees and other closing costs.

✗ Forgetting to schedule walk-throughs. If you find damage or any new problems with the home after you've taken possession, it may be difficult to get the previous owner to fix them at their cost.

7

Maybe It's a "Money Pit"— But It's *Your*

Money Pit

---

*Y*ou have the keys and are standing in your new home. It's bare. Where to begin? Do you need new furniture? Should you renovate the bathroom right away? How does the garden look?

A new home means a lot of choices, and a lot of responsibility. In this chapter I'll talk about preparing yourself for home ownership, including first steps, budgeting and then the fun stuff—buying furnishings, garden shrubs, and other things to make that house a home.

Karen, the teacher in Burford, Ontario, was sure she was ready for the costs of home ownership. After all, she had budgeted for all the expenses: mortgage, taxes, utilities and insurance. She had also factored in her other regular expenses, including gym membership, car insurance and groceries. She even set aside some money in case of emergencies.

What she didn't bargain for were all the other little expenses that can add up when you own a home, including buying a ladder, garden hose, lawn mower, extension cords and cleaning supplies. Karen describes it as "all that stuff you were used to having around the house when you rented or lived at home."

Those costs don't even include the decorating and other upgrades she wants eventually to do in her home, including adding central air conditioning.

"You see what your parents have or your older siblings and you want your house to be perfect when you move in. That's fine if you can afford it, but for me it means I have to save money first, and be patient," Karen says. "I find it helps to write a list, set goals and realize what you can handle. Then do one thing at a time."

Esther, who has bought two houses on her own in Toronto, agrees that pacing yourself is best when you first move into your new home. "Be willing to make changes slowly," advises Esther, while slowly chipping away at the flaking stain on her deck in the house she bought a couple of years ago.

Susan, who got the great deal on the condo in Toronto's Rosedale area, extends that advice to include worries about paying off the debt. "My brother gave me some good advice when I first bought my own place. He said, 'For the first two years, just make it your home and make it nice. Don't worry so much about paying down the mortgage.' I think that's good advice."

That said, other homebuyers, such as Adriana, whom you'll hear from later in this chapter, prefer to set up their homes right away, and get on with life. It all depends on your personality and preferences.

Before you make even that first mortgage payment, there are some initial steps you need to take when you move into your newly purchased home. These include making the home safe and making it comfortable.

Let's start with safety.

Safety First

The very first thing Ruth, the Hamilton-based artist, did when she got the keys to her new home was change the locks. In fact, not only did she change the locks, she changed the doors. "I wouldn't stay there by myself until I had those replaced with more solid doors," says Ruth. "I had to feel safe."

Changing the locks is the first thing many single woman do when they buy a new home. The locksmith was the first to see each of my new homes, long before some of my friends were invited. And if the home comes with a security system, you'll want to have it reset and change the password. Even if the sellers were a sweet old couple who reminded you of your grandparents, you don't know who their children are. Maybe they had to sell that place to bail their son (or daughter) out of jail!

All kidding aside, you will have more peace of mind if you update the security in your home. This includes ensuring that all windows lock. If you don't have a security system, invest in one. It's an investment in yourself because you'll feel safe, but also because you'll pay less insurance since insurers give discounts to homeowners with security systems.

It's also a good idea to ensure there is good outdoor lighting around your house for when you come home late at night. This is true for condos as well. If you feel the lighting outside your building is poor, talk to the condo board about what can be done.

The Toronto loft I bought, in a building that was newly converted to condos, had a second entrance on a dark back street. That entrance was also partially covered, and some of the other owners parked their cars nearby. Unfortunately, because it was a dark, out of the way street, it was also where the local street kids went to shoot drugs or have sex. (It's true. You wonder now why I moved yet again?) Within the first few months of occupancy, some of those cars were broken into—one even in the middle of a sunny summer day. It wasn't long before the condo board agreed to put up brighter lights at the back of the building, and eventually security cameras.

There are other ways to make sure your home is safe from the start. Here's a list of things to take care of almost immediately:

- ✓ Decide on a fire evacuation plan. Think about—and write down—the quickest and shortest way to get out of the home in case of fire.

- ✓ Buy fire extinguishers (or, in a condo, find out where they are). If you have more than one floor in the home, put one on each level. Once you've got them, check them once a year.

- ✓ Install smoke detectors and carbon monoxide detectors. These are legal requirements in most areas now. Make sure you have both, and keep the batteries charged.

- ✓ Keep a list of emergency numbers handy. Put 911, and other emergency numbers, on your speed dial.

Budgeting for Real Life

Now that you're securely in your new home you will need to make sure you have a budget. There are dozens of homeowner expenses to prepare for, from the mortgage, utilities, taxes and condo fees (if applicable), to regular maintenance and repair costs for services such as security alarm systems and maybe paying the neighbour's kid to cut the lawn.

There is also the "just in case" cash you need to set aside for emergencies such as plumbing backups or a leaky roof. Even if you are able to fix some or all of these on your own, your home ages and may require major repairs at some point. Experts suggest setting aside 5 percent of your take-home pay in a "just in case" account. That way, if disaster strikes, you won't have to scramble to come up with the cash.

Barb, the single thirty-something who bought a home on half an acre of land in Georgetown, Ontario, says even though she had a home inspection that pointed out a few costly repairs, she wasn't ready for the surprise expenses. One of those expenses included replacing the septic system, including the septic bed, for a cost of $30,000. Another surprise was the new pool liner she need at a price tag of about $2,000.

There is also the cost of snow removal in the winter, cutting the grass in the summer, insurance and regular maintenance. Luckily, Barb is able to borrow a colleague's husband to do small chores such as cleaning the eavestroughs and hanging Christmas lights. "In a condo all you have to do is change the furnace filter. With an older house—and everyone warned me about this—you have to be prepared for a lot of surprises, especially in the country." Barb also warns that "every renovation costs more than the quote."

Don't Count Out Condos

Condos are not immune to costly repairs. Susan, who earlier in this chapter passed on her brother's advice about mortgage payments, found out a month after moving into her Rosedale condo that the aging building's roof needed replacing. Because her condo building was constructed in the 1950s, it requires regular upkeep. Not only did the roof have to be replaced after water from a rainstorm gushed down walls in some units, but the balconies were rotting and the windows needed replacing.

The condo board decided to do a lot of repairs at once, and because the cost was much more than what was set aside in the reserve fund, they agreed on a special assessment. This is a one-of-a-kind charge imposed to meet large expenditures that cannot be covered in the reserve fund.

How did Susan react? "I wrote a cheque and didn't paint for 10 months," Susan says of the bill. Susan and her fellow tenants in that building will also make lump sum payments for a few years to pay off those renovations. "On the bright side, the value of my property has almost doubled since then," Susan says, adding that, just like a home, a condo building needs to be maintained.

While not all major home repairs can be prevented, doing regular maintenance and handling small repairs right away can help you avoid more costly ones down the road. It's not unlike those preventative visits to the dentist to avoid more pain and expense in the long term.

You've already been through the home inspection process, but there will still be some things to learn about your home. You have to spend some time getting to know your home to understand its wants and needs. The Canada Mortgage and Housing Corporation has outlined some of the basic but important ways of looking at your home, how it's put together, and what it needs.

- Your home is made up of various components that work together. These include mechanical systems (heating, air conditioning and ventilation) and the building envelope (foundations, floors, walls, windows, doors and roof).
- You need to learn enough about the major mechanical systems of your home to be able to perform routine maintenance and handle various emergencies. Every adult member of your household should know the location of the following: main shutoff valves for water and fuel; emergency switch for the furnace or burner; hot water heater thermostat; main electrical switch; fuse box or circuit breaker box.

- Renovations targeted at increasing energy efficiency (such as extra insulation) may affect appliances that exhaust by a chimney. Check chimney performance if you tighten the envelope or add exhaust fans.
- Moisture, heat and air pressure must be balanced to ensure a healthy home.

(Source: Canada Mortgage and Housing Corporation. For a detailed list of maintenance checks by season, check out CMHC's lists online: http://www.cmhc.ca/en/co/maho/gemare/gemare_003.cfm)

The Fun Spending

Now that we've discussed the money you have to spend, let's move on to the money you want to spend. It doesn't matter how tight-fisted you are, you will want to decorate that new home. Even if you are moving from another house, every home has its own character that you will want to match with your personality—and that will mean some new purchases.

Furniture is one of those wants to consider. Personal finance celebrity Suze Orman says you should factor this into your costs when saving for a new home. "If you think the furniture you have in your rental is going to make you happy in your own home, you are doing some interesting drugs," she wrote in one of her online columns. "I can guarantee you that all the old hand-me-down furniture that worked great in your rental isn't going to psychologically cut it in your new digs. Sure, for a while it may suffice, but over time all those well-placed ads will get the better of you, and you're going to want to go on a furniture-buying binge."

She warns against the "interest-free for one year" furniture sales. "You charge and charge until your home is full of new furniture to impress your friends. And in the process you pile up a ton of credit card or consumer loan debt. Congratulations, you have just put yourself in a serious 'small' debt bind at the same time you have committed to the biggest financial responsibility of your life: the mortgage."

Her advice extends to buying that new car, new linens, dishes and small appliances. It's too early to be keeping up with the Joneses—after all, you just moved in! Instead, Suze recommends you take your time: "Just date your house for a while before you get married to it. This means that while you are getting to know your new home, just live in it with what you currently have. See what rooms you like the best. Observe where the sun hits. Think through what kind of furniture you would like and then just do it one room at a time, so you can pay the bill without running up a balance on your credit card. Trust me, it's better to not have a new designer chair to sit in, than no money to live on."

Adriana, the Toronto television producer who talked about safe space in Chapter Three, set aside a chunk of cash to pay for furnishing her 600-square-foot, two-storey space. Her plan was to furnish it as quickly as she, and her wallet, could handle. "All I came into my loft with was my computer, clock radio, clothes and toiletries. And I managed to do it just fine with a little bit of cash to spare," she says.

Her biggest challenge was finding furniture to fit. "I was admittedly overwhelmed by the underwhelming amount of space I had to work with. I had to find furniture that was multi-functional, meaning it had to double as storage since my 600-square-foot pad had little of that."

Adriana turned to her designer (also known as her boyfriend) to help her choose and assemble the furniture for her new home. In fact, she recalls, they almost broke up over how to assemble the Ikea dresser. "It was stressful because I grew up in the West where there's lots of space. The houses are all fairly big and I never once saw my parents have to consider things like: 'Will I be able to walk through the living room without bumping into things?'"

Apart from the furniture, Adriana realized she had to fork over money for a lot of other expenses, including a ceiling fan and having custom blinds installed for her 18-foot floor-to-ceiling windows. "It's great living in a small space and in a unique space, but some of its attributes have specialized costs associated with them," Adriana warns.

Dayna, the thirty-something Vancouver lawyer who bought a townhouse in that city, says one expense she doesn't regret was hiring an interior designer. While it may seem like an extravagant expense, Dayna says when you are starting from scratch a designer can keep you from making mistakes even before you start decorating. "I think she saved me more money than she cost me," says Dayna. What's more, Dayna says the designer was able to get her discounts from suppliers.

Dayna thinks the designer made the process a lot easier for her as a single woman. "I was going into the project without a spouse to bounce ideas off. Whenever I had a question I would call my designer. When you are spending that kind of money it's helpful to know what you are doing. Hiring her was great—one of the best decisions I made in that process."

If you own a house, as opposed to a condo, you also have to think about the outside of your home. Remember the garden isn't just for you, it's for the neighbours and the neighbourhood to enjoy as well. That doesn't mean you should consult the old man next door as to what flowers to plant and where to place the lawn furniture, but remember that your neighbours have to look at your yard, and vice versa. Even if your neighbours don't like you, they shouldn't hate your front lawn.

Kathy, the City of Toronto employee, says it's a good idea to make friends with the neighbours, especially as a single woman. "You'll want to be on their good side, especially when you want to ask the couple next door to watch your house while you are on vacation."

One way to make friends with the neighbours is to keep your property tidy. "Neighbours appreciate it if you make an effort with your front lawn," says Kathy. "They like that kind of stuff."

That said, Kathy says she doesn't spend countless hours working on her home, either inside or out. Just like Esther and Susan, whom you heard from at the start of this chapter, Kathy cautions single women homebuyers to take their time when it comes to tackling house-related projects of all kinds. "Don't spend every weekend doing chores around the house. Pace yourself. Do one big project a year."

The danger of taking on too much is that you can burn out, and then possibly resent that property. Says Kathy, "I don't let my house own me. I don't stay at home all the time and do projects. I go on vacation."

Again, do what best suits your personality and lifestyle.

Budgeting: The Whole Story

I've cautioned you on the dozens of expenses, beyond the mortgage payments, that come with home ownership. If you have never been on a budget, now (before you buy a home) might be a good time to start tracking your spending. Below is a suggested list of costs that you'll need to budget for if you want to own and maintain a home. Of course, the expenses depend on your property, lifestyle and personal tastes, but consider this guide from our friends at CMHC to get you started.

Household Budget as a Homeowner

Housing Expenses

✓ Electricity

✓ Heating

✓ Mortgage (principal and interest)

✓ Parking fees (if paid separately)

✓ Property insurance

✓ Property taxes

✓ Water

✓ Property and contents insurance

Non-Housing Expenses

✓ Cable TV/satellite/video rental

✓ Car fuel

✓ Car lease/loan payments

✓ Car insurance and licence

✓ Car repairs and service

✓ Charitable donations

✓ Child care

✓ Child support/alimony

✓ Clothes

✓ Dental expenses

✓ Entertainment, recreation, movies

✓ Furnishings

✓ Groceries

✓ Life insurance

✓ Lunches/eating out

✓ Medical expenses, prescriptions, eyewear

✓ Newspapers, magazines, books

✓ Personal items

✓ Public transportation

✓ Savings (bank account, RRSPs)

✓ Telephone

✓ Other expenses

Total Monthly Expenses = $

(Source: Canada Mortgage and Housing Corporation)

Checklist: Now That You've Moved In

✓ Pace yourself. You have plenty of time to renovate, redecorate and pay down the mortgage. Get to know your home before you start making changes.

✓ Safety first. Secure your home: change the locks; get a security system; make sure the windows and doors close and lock securely.

✓ Maintenance is key. Replace the batteries in the fire alarm. Check the fire extinguisher. Don't forget the larger parts of the home, such as the roof, and mechanicals, such as the furnace.

✓ Budget. Need furniture to fill that home? How about window coverings and an air purifying system? Plan and save for these items so that you aren't overwhelmed by their compounding costs when you move in.

✓ Make friends with the neighbours. Like them or not, you never know when you might need them.

Common Mistakes to Avoid:

✗ Rushing to buy new furniture and fixtures. Date your home for a while, as Suze Orman suggests. Figure out what you need and what you want, and buy the needs first.

✗ Not saving enough. You have to set money aside for both maintenance and emergencies.

✗ Worrying about paying down the mortgage right away. Instead, enjoy your home for a while first.

8

Renovate
Right

$\mathcal{D}$oing regular maintenance on your house is one thing, but you may wish to delve a bit deeper to help improve the value of your home. Maybe you bought a "handyman's special," and are prepared to call in the contractors before you move in. Or maybe you've lived in that home for a while and want to refresh the kitchen, bathroom, or another room to make it a more pleasant place for you to live. Whatever your reasons for renovating, be aware that renovations are costly, time-consuming, and require a lot of preparation before you starting taking down walls and ripping up floors.

Esther, whom you met previously and who has bought a few homes on her own, says she has been through a few renovation projects. "It's a hassle. I slept in my basement for three months during the last one. And before that, it was four years of renovations." But for her, the advantage was having her home changed to suit her lifestyle and personal tastes. "I always compare it to having a baby. Once the pain of labour is over, you have a lifetime to enjoy it," Esther says.

What's more, renovations will almost always increase the value of your home. According to the Appraisal Institute of Canada, bathroom renovation projects provide the highest payback for potential homeowners. Kitchen renovations came second in the 2004 survey, while painting (both interior and exterior) was third.

Below is the average payback range for some of the most common household renovations:

- kitchen (75-100%)
- bathroom (75-100%)
- interior painting (50-100%)
- exterior painting (50-100%)
- window or door replacement (50-75%)
- finished basement (50-75%)

One of the biggest fears single women have when it comes to hiring a contractor is getting scammed. Mike Holmes, of the renovation television program *Holmes on Homes*, says nobody should fear getting taken by renovators if they follow three basic rules:

1. Be patient.

"Having patience to find the right contractor is first and foremost," Mike says. It's a big project and will potentially cost a lot of money. You want to invest time in your investment.

2. Educate yourself.

"The more you educate yourself, the more confident you will be," Mike says. This includes learning everything you can about your home, consulting books and magazines and talking to others who have done renovation projects. It's also imperative that you check with your local municipality to find out whether a building permit is needed for your project.

3. Check out the contractor.

"Ask them how long they've been in the business. What do they specialize in? How many references can they provide?" Mike says. The more references, the better, he says, and suggests homeowners call all of them. He says homeowners should ask previous clients questions such as, "Did they start on time? Were they courteous? Were there any nasty surprises?" Red flags should go up if you hear that a contractor doesn't do what he says he will. (More on finding a contractor later in this chapter.)

"You're the boss," Mike says. "Stick to what you believe in. Control the job. It doesn't mean yell or scream. You should be making a friendship with your contractor, but stand your ground, and keep smiling."

- - - -

Kathryn, a fifty-something market research consultant in Toronto, says she could barely change a light bulb when she decided to take on her first renovation project. "I didn't know anything about construction," recalls Kathryn, who bought a duplex in Toronto's west end with four rooms and two kitchens.

She turned up her nose at the house when she first saw it. After all, as a single woman, she certainly didn't need two kitchens. But when the house price dropped by $20,000 she reconsidered. Kathryn was assured it wasn't much work to remove the second kitchen—which she did after deciding to buy the home and renovate it.

In fact, there were a lot of problems with the house when she bought it. First, there was that extra kitchen to be removed. There was also the outdated bathroom and the unfinished basement with a mildew smell that filled the house. Because she was prepared to renovate, Kathryn got a great deal. "It was probably my lack of knowledge about renovations that led to my buying the house," she recalls. "If I had known what it involved, I would have been too scared to buy the house. Because I got the house cheap it allowed me the time and money to do those repairs."

The renovations cost about $50,000. While that may seem like a lot, it has helped increase the value of her home significantly. What's more, the renovations she did were to her tastes. Kathryn's only regret was that she did the work in stages, without really knowing how one change might impact another. "I wish I had had the foresight to think myself through the process. Part of it is not knowing what to do, part of it takes experience and time. I wish I had been able to figure out how to do it all at once, not piecemeal."

Not planning ahead is one of the biggest mistakes people make when tackling a renovation, and it can cost you.

David, a reputable Toronto-based contractor, says a lot of renovation projects go over budget because the homeowner didn't think ahead and tried to make changes in the middle of a project. "Changes on the go are going to slaughter you financially," David says. "The contractor and the crew take pride in what they do and when you walk in and say, 'Just move that over six inches' … We hate that." Changes to the plans take more time, and therefore more money.

David says many people, both men and women, single and married, need the help of a professional architect or designer to plan a renovation.

He says too many homeowners believe they can plan their project based on watching a lot of renovation programs on television. "There is a good saying that a little knowledge is a dangerous thing," says David. "I don't know how many times I hear people say, 'I was watching Mike Holmes and Mike did this, or Mike did that.' Well, Mike is on TV."

Just as Mike Holmes does with his television clients, David says that he and other contractors often end up educating clients on the particulars of their renovation. He says a good contractor is happy to do this. However, when it comes to personal taste, only the client can tell the contractor what's best.

More about finding a contractor and other steps to take before embarking on a renovation project later in this chapter. First, let's talk about getting you focussed on the renovation itself.

Why Renovate?

Long before the hammering begins, you should sit down and think about why you are renovating. Is your kitchen out of date? Is the layout wrong for your lifestyle? How do you plan to use the bathroom not just the day after it's fixed up, but two to ten years later, if you plan to be in the house that long? You don't need a crystal ball to plan renovations, but you do need to be aware of the space, and what you want out of it. Renovating is another commitment you are making in the home ownership process. So think carefully before you get too involved.

Some factors to consider:

- Use of space. How you use a room determines the amount of space required and the extent to which the space needs to be open or closed to surrounding areas of your home. What activities will take place in the room? What existing or future furnishings must fit into it? Will noise from this room be disruptive to others?

- Light and brightness. What are the lighting requirements of the activities planned for each room? Do existing windows provide adequate sunlight and a feeling of spaciousness? Will you use this room more during the day or in the evening? If artificial light is needed, would general lighting or task lighting be more suitable?
- Movement of people. What are the traffic patterns through each area of your home? Does a room provide access to other frequently used parts of your home, such as the kitchen or bathroom, and does this conflict with the activities you plan for this room?

(Source: Canadian Home Builders' Association)

Where to Begin

The choices of what you can do with your home can be overwhelming. And though you might have started thinking about a renovation because you fell in love with certain kitchen cabinets or countertops or tiles, those are minor choices—and relatively minor expenses—in the scope of the whole renovation. The far bigger costs in renovations are often behind the walls, with mechanicals, plumbing, electrical, and sometimes even structural changes. While choosing finishes is important (and fun), it should be seen as just one step in the whole renovation. Get started thinking about finishes early on so that you're sure of your choices when it's time to place orders, but be prepared for lots of other, far less glamorous, choices along the way.

As David mentioned earlier, many people hire an architect or designer to help them work through a renovation project. It will cost more, but there is also the argument that it can save you money. For instance, if you pick kitchen cupboards on your own, then decide after they are installed that they don't work, you'll pay a lot more to have them replaced than if you had hired a professional to bypass the error in the first place.

Architects and designers also work directly with the contractors and can often spot possibilities a homeowner cannot, such as taking down a wall (and knowing if additional structural support is needed when you do!). The same goes for layout and design; a designer will notice if kitchen cupboards are going to block appliances, or if closets and doorways are being constructed in awkward locations.

What's more, a designer can spot problem workmanship on the part of a contractor that a homeowner may not realize until well after the work is finished. David, the contractor you met earlier, says the smoothest projects are those that involve a designer or architect. "The ideal situation is when the homeowner has hired an architect they trust, they give that project to the architect and between the client and the architect they have hammered out the details of the project. We don't have a lot to do with the client in these situations; we deal with the architect or designer. This is best because we speak the same language. The communication is more effective. Then the customer comes in, writes me a cheque and we're on our way to the next project."

That said, David says the most common circumstance is that the client hires the contractor with a concept and leaves it up to them to carry it out. When that happens, he says the best way to keep costs down is to be clear about what you want. "It's a very emotional business, but it's best to take the emotion out," David adds.

Dayna, the Vancouver lawyer, says because she couldn't afford a newly renovated home in that city she looked for places with "good bones" that she could renovate. She bought her current townhome because she liked the neighbourhood and the layout, and felt it had potential. "I had a vision of what I could do with it," Dayna explains.

After examining dozens of decor magazines, Dayna put her vision on paper. She then hired professionals to help her execute that vision. A cabinet and furniture maker helped her redesign the kitchen; flooring professionals advised her on the floors; and an interior designer helped her choose materials and other decor. "She was enormously helpful that way and had some really good advice and tips," Dayna says of the designer. "As a person doing this on my own, it was really nice to have someone to consult who knew what she was doing. It made the whole process a little less overwhelming and scary."

Finding a Renovator

Whether you're looking for a general contractor, interior designer or cabinet maker, you want to choose the right professional to help you get the job done. References are key. Just as you did to find your real estate agent, lender and lawyer, you'll want references for a renovator. You will be spending a lot of money to work with whomever you choose, so you only want to hire skilled professionals who will give you the most for your dollar. Remember, too, that the people you hire may be in your home even when you aren't. In some cases, for major renovations, they will likely have your keys. They will also be using your washroom when nature calls and maybe even your telephone in case of emergency. You need to hire people you feel you can trust, especially as a single woman.

"Customers have to be secure with us being in their homes," says David. "It's a huge thing to be in someone's home. You have to invade their space, take it over, destroy it—and they are hoping you will put it back together again. The anxiety level from the start is huge." David recommends that homeowners, especially single women, ask the contractor about all the people doing the work, whether they are part of his full-time crew, or sub-contractors that he hires regularly. "You want a contractor where the same guys are showing up at your home each morning—a familiar face, someone you can talk to. You want someone who carries the continuity of the project and knows the problems and pitfalls."

You also need to book ahead. In good economic times, a good renovator will have worked lined up well in advance, says David, up to six months or even more. "In a hot reno market, anyone worth their weight is booked." That said, David says you want to ensure the contractor is focussed on your project when it's your turn. "You don't want a contractor that is stretched too thin."

After you've collected a few names from friends, agents or colleagues, you want to interview them before choosing who to hire. Here are some tips from the CHBA on what to look for. The tips are specific to renovators, but can be applied to any professional you hire to help renovate your home:

- **Presentation.** Professional renovators operate in a businesslike manner. They respect your schedule and show up for appointments on time. They present themselves well, are organized and deal with your questions and concerns directly. They earn your confidence because they follow through on promises—if they say they will call you back tomorrow, they do. How a renovator deals with you before a contract is signed tells you a lot about how you can expect to be treated once the job begins.

- **Communication.** Renovation is a "people business" and good renovators are good listeners and communicators. Professional renovators must "translate" your ideas and goals into a workable plan and a pleasant experience. This requires a solid working relationship and good rapport. If you're not comfortable with renovators you interview or don't feel you can communicate with them effectively, you should keep looking to find the right person for your job.

- **Skills and experience.** Renovating a home can be a far more complex task than building it in the first place. It takes years of experience in the business before most renovators are ready to manage a major project on their own. It also involves a lot of different types of work, some of which require specialized expertise. Whatever the scope and nature of your project, your renovator needs to have solid experience with that type of work. They also need to prove to you that they do.

- **Professional reputation.** Established renovators will provide you with references from previous customers, and in fact, you shouldn't even have to ask for them. They also work with a network of other businesses within your community—banks, material suppliers and trades. It's a good idea to ask a renovator for references to any of these people to find out about their reputation within the industry itself.

(Source: Canadian Home Builders' Association)

Liz, the divorced travel consultant from Chapter Two, encountered a couple of problems when she hired a contractor to replace the floors in her home. She took a recommendation from a friend and compared quotes with other contractors before choosing who to hire. "The good part was that I could trust him 100 percent with the keys to my house," says Liz. "The bad part was that I didn't know he was doing other jobs at the same time."

This meant Liz's renovation was delayed because the contractor had too many other projects on the go. What's more, he fixed other problems in her house she didn't ask for, and then charged her for it.

Get It in Writing

As a homeowner, you need to be clear with the contractors from the start about what is included in the project. This is where a contract comes in handy. Even if the contractor doesn't present you with one, you can draw one up on your own.

The CHBA recommends the following elements for any renovator contract:

- The parties to the contract (i.e., you and the renovation contractor), including their street addresses, telephone and fax numbers, email addresses and the renovator's business or GST number.
- The contract documents. The contract form must also identify all attachments such as: drawings/blueprints/plans; specifications (description of work and a precise list of materials and products, including types, brands, grades, thickness, colour, model); other documents signed by both parties in the course of the contract (e.g., change order forms).
- Description of work to be done by the renovator, and also work not to be done under the contract, or to be done by you or others outside the terms of the contract.
- Start and completion dates often include a statement indicating that the renovator cannot be responsible for delays due to circumstances beyond the renovator's control, changes to the work, and so on.
- Terms of payment set out the total amount of the contract and a payment schedule: deposit upon signing the contract, how and when the remainder will be paid (at regular intervals or specific milestones), and the treatment of taxes.
- Holdbacks are a provincial legislative requirement that protect you against subcontractors who may place a lien on your property in the event the renovation contractor doesn't pay them. On each payment you make to your renovator, you must hold back a certain percentage for a specified length of time. For more details, check out www.HiringAContractor.com.
- Changes in work once the renovation is in progress (also called extras and deletions) must be written up as "change orders," signed

by both parties and attached to the contract. Any change to the contract price and schedule should be clearly noted on the order.

- Allowances refer to a lump sum in the contract price, allocated for items to be selected directly by the homeowners, such as flooring, fixtures or cabinets.

- Contingencies (sometimes called a "contingency budget") refer to an amount set aside to deal with the unexpected or items that the renovator cannot gauge accurately until work is in progress. If not needed, you won't be invoiced for it.

- Standards of work describe the renovator's commitment to performing the work in accordance with the contract documents and in a diligent and workmanlike manner with minimum inconvenience to your household, to protect your property as well as neighbouring properties and to comply with regulatory requirements. Includes responsibility for daily clean-up.

- The renovator's liability insurance (minimum $1 million) and workers' compensation coverage must be paid up to date and proof of coverage provided and attached to the contract.

- Municipal and/or utility permits, inspections and approvals are usually arranged by professional renovators as part of their service—but note that homeowners are ultimately responsible for complying with these regulations. The contract should specify who is going to obtain them.

- The renovator's warranty describes what is covered and for how long. It should include a statement of the contractor's intent to hand over manufacturers' product warranties to you upon completion of work.

- Subcontractors scheduled to work on your home may be listed.

(Source: Canadian Home Builders' Association)

The Canada Mortgage and Housing Corporation also has some advice for a renovator-homeowner contract.

- Use of facilities and utilities should be outlined: water, electricity, washroom and storage for materials.
- Signage: A statement that you will permit the contractor to display a promotional sign on your property during the project.
- Dispute resolution in the event of a conflict. This may include the name of a third party arbitrator, or state that both parties will agree to binding arbitration.

Financing the Renovation

If you have saved up the money for renovations, good for you. A great many people, however, need to finance the changes, which usually means borrowing money from your bank.

You have a few different options.

- Personal line of credit. This is one of the most popular financing options for smaller renovations and is also ideal for ongoing or long-term renovations. With one application, you establish a revolving credit line that you can access at any time, up to your approved limit. An itemized monthly statement lets you keep track of your renovation expenses, and you only pay interest on the funds you use. As you pay off your balance, you can re-borrow the unused funds without reapplying. And you'll always enjoy a rate that's lower than most personal loans and credit cards.
- Personal loan. An installment loan lets you budget regular payments at a fixed or variable interest rate for a set period of time. Repayment periods typically vary from one to five years. However, once you pay off your loan, you no longer have access to the credit

and will have to go through the approval process again if you need to borrow more funds.

- Secured lines of credit and home equity loan plans. These lines of credit and personal loan plans are secured by the equity in your home and are among the most economical ways to fund a renovation if you have built up equity in your home. They have all the advantages of the unsecured versions, but offer preferred interest rates. While there is typically no cost to open a secured line of credit or home equity loan plan, legal and appraisal fees usually apply.

- Homeowner mortgage. If you have an existing mortgage, it can be advantageous to refinance it, particularly if you're planning a major renovation and want to spread the cost over a long period. You may be able to borrow up to 90% of the value of your home, less the outstanding balance of any existing mortgage. This option allows you to take advantage of mortgage rates, which are often substantially lower than credit card and loan rates. Loans of 75% or more of the appraised value of your home must be insured against borrower default; the mortgage insurance premium can be paid up front or added to the mortgage amount.

(Source: Canada Mortgage and Housing Corporation)

When you're determining how much you'll need for your renovation, remember to leave room for the cost overruns that often happen. Those with experience often recommend allowing at least 10 percent, and as much as 25 percent, of the total renovation budget. (This is sometimes called a "contingency budget," and was mentioned in the list of what you should include in a contract.)

You'll also want to think about basic decorating costs. Once you have a new bathroom, living room, or kitchen, you'll likely be tempted to redecorate those rooms (new towels, curtains, artwork, extra furniture), so having extra money set aside will help you enjoy the new space sooner.

Building Permits

Before you start ripping apart that living room, you probably need to get a building permit. Not all renovations require one, but it's best to check with your municipal zoning office to see if your project needs a permit. If you don't, and the municipality finds out about the project, they can shut it down until they get more information. This means putting your contractors on hold, and possibly even paying them while they play cards on your lawn waiting for the city to make its decision.

It's your legal responsibility as the homeowner to get building permits, not the people doing the work, but it's most often the contractor who actually obtains the permit. Sounds confusing, I know, but what this means, in practice, is that the contractor will usually go down to City Hall and get the permit. But if he fails to do so, the law sees you, the homeowner, as the one responsible. Make sure all permits are in place before the work begins.

Why are building permits necessary? They're definitely more than another tax by the government. Building permits ensure that your plans are in line with other municipal requirements, such as zoning regulations and heritage building designations. Even more importantly, a building permit is not granted unless your plans show that any renovations will meet the basic health, safety and structural requirements outlined in each province's building code.

According to CMHC, a building permit is generally required for renovations that involve changes to the structure or systems of your home. These include:

- new additions
- reconfiguration of space by moving or removing walls
- new window and door openings
- installation of fireplaces

You may also need to obtain separate electrical and plumbing permits, depending on the type of work you are having done. Your municipality will let you know when you go to apply for the initial building permit.

Some renovations may not require a permit. These include:

- re-roofing
- painting
- re-siding
- flooring and/or cabinet installation (unless the structural subfloor [joists] must be changed)
- window and door replacement (if the size remains the same)

It's best to check with your municipality to find out if a permit is required for your renovation. To do this, bring information on your renovation project, including a scale floor plan, when you make a visit to your municipal planning office. For larger-scale projects you should bring all plan drawings, as well as a site survey. It also helps to bring letters from neighbours supporting your renovation project. This proves to the municipality that the community around you is aware and accepting of the project and won't likely call to complain about any impact the work may have on their property, such as noise (hammering or drilling), smell (in the case of tar roofing, for example) or obstructions on the street (garbage bins or trucks). The goal is to do the renovation with as little disruption to the neighbours as possible.

Renovating your home is expensive, stressful and requires a lot of planning. But at the end of the day, the changes you envision will not only make your home more comfortable for you, but will likely increase its value. Every renovation project has its own set of requirements and potential drawbacks. The Canadian Renovators' Council has put together a list of "golden rules" for renovating that should also help you with your project. See below:

Golden Rules of Renovation

- Know what you want. Take the time you need to explore the possibilities for your home and develop a firm plan. Begin with the fundamentals: what you need and how you want your "new" home to look, feel and work for you and your family. Once you have a clear idea of the "big picture," your renovator will help you work out all the details.

- Set a realistic budget. Decide as early as possible how much money you want to spend. This allows you and your renovator to focus on the work that can be done within that budget. Experienced renovators can provide sound cost advice and recommendations. Sit down with your lender and discuss the amount you can reasonably afford and the most suitable financing options. Remember that your budget should cover everything that may arise from the renovation, including such items as new drapery, blinds, furniture and appliances.

- Plan for the long term. Thinking ahead avoids short-term renovations that may need to be redone in the future. Discuss your short- and long-term goals openly with your renovator. Professional renovators can conduct a thorough inspection of your home and offer suggestions for the most effective sequencing of work over a period of time.

- Don't jeopardize the quality of your renovation by compromising on the quality of products or materials. If it's worth doing, it's worth doing well, and that means using products that offer the right combination of performance, durability and aesthetics. Experienced renovators can help you choose the best products within your budget.

- Don't choose a renovator on price alone. While it is always tempting to go for the lowest price, you need to consider the implications of doing so. Does the renovator understand what's involved in your project and have the necessary experience? Will the renovator offer a warranty on the work? Will the renovator still be in business if you need to call back?

- Protect yourself. Dealing with a professional renovator is your greatest protection against an incompetent or unfinished job. A written contract spells out the arrangements between you and your renovator and describes your renovation in detail. Professional renovators also carry workers' compensation, liability insurance and any licences required by your province.

- Don't buy from a door-to-door salesperson without carefully checking out the company. Before you enter into any kind of agreement, talk with friends and family. Contact your local Home Builders' Association to see if the company is a member: membership is an indication of professionalism. Also check with the Better Business Bureau to see if anyone has lodged a complaint against the company.

(Source: Canadian Renovators' Council)

Another spin on how to successfully plan a renovation comes from experienced homeowners themselves. The Canadian Home Builders' Association has compiled a list of advice based on interviews with people who have had renovations done to their homes.

Advice from Homeowners

- Find a renovator you can trust and are comfortable with. This is crucial to a good renovation experience. You need to check out the renovator thoroughly. Ask lots of questions when you meet. Talk with previous customers. Visit past or current projects; you want to feel that "if the renovator did something like that in my home, I'd be very happy." You also need to be confident that the company is financially stable and will be around in the future. And while it may be hard to define a comfortable personal fit, you need to feel "in your gut" that you can trust and work well with this person.

- Find out what services the renovator offers, at the early planning stage. Homeowners often don't realize that many professional renovation contractors also provide design and planning services. Even if you want to work with a designer or architect of your own choosing, a contractor can add a lot of value to the process. "Our renovator saw opportunities for improving our design and offered alternative solutions to structural challenges, saving us money in the process," says one homeowner.

- Make sure you have a detailed written contract. "We chose the renovator who had it all written out. We knew what we were in for and didn't have to lie awake at night worrying what the final costs would be."

- Know the facts before the work begins. What does the work entail? How will it be done and by whom? How will it affect your day-to-day living? Should you consider moving out? What if you have questions or want to make changes? The more you know up front about the whole process, the less anxious you'll feel.

- Take an active role throughout the project. "It's your investment and your home, so you want to follow things closely and know what's going on at all times." The best results come from good communication and a good working relationship between you and your renovator. A good renovator provides regular, if not daily, updates and is easy to get hold of if you have questions or concerns. You should be prepared to spend time going over drawings, monitoring the progress of your project, and discussing decisions with your renovator.

- Don't expect a problem-free renovation. The bigger the project, the more likely you will run into the unexpected, such as existing deficiencies hidden in the walls, delays in special orders, or bad weather. Be flexible and understand that some things are beyond the renovator's or your control. "If there is good rapport and trust between you and your renovator, it is usually easy to find a solution and move beyond the problem."

- Plan ahead for your finishes. Typically, homeowners are responsible for choosing cabinets, flooring, tiles, fixtures and the many other finishes that will complete the job. This can be time-consuming. As one homeowner says, "My afternoon at the bath showroom turned into two full days." Set aside plenty of time and begin early. In some markets, there may be a significant delay for special orders. And take full advantage of your renovator's experience to help you find the best options.

- Keep money in reserve for extras. Once the work begins, it is not uncommon for homeowners to want to go an extra step—a better quality tile, brand new appliances and so on. "Once you are into it, you realize that just so-so is not good enough, and that now is the best time to get those extra little touches of style or luxury."

Checklist: If and When You Renovate

✓ Be prepared. Hire an architect or designer if necessary and within your budget.

✓ Get references. Any professional you hire to do your home renovation should come with references. You should also ask to see their work, in particular recent jobs.

✓ Expect delays. Renovations take time. You need to fit this project into your lifestyle and be prepared for the inconvenience. Keep thinking about the finished project.

✓ Visit the municipal planning (zoning) office. Tell them about your project and find out if you need a building permit.

Common Mistakes to Avoid:

✗ Not being organized. Nothing slows down a renovation more than a homeowner who cannot make up her mind.

✗ Making frequent changes in the middle of a renovation. This is certain to cause a jump in the costs of your renovation. Remember that renovators are working off the initial plan you gave them.

✗ Not getting or checking references. If the renovation from one company is half the price of the other two, be skeptical. Check references. There are renovation scams out there, just like there are in any business. Checking references should eliminate your chances of getting "taken" by a contractor. Don't be the dummy that didn't do her homework, only to regret it thousands of dollars later.

✗ Forgetting to get a permit. You've worked hard to pay for this new kitchen. You don't want to find out halfway through that you needed a permit to replace that front window, only to have the project put on indefinite hold.

✗ Not drawing up a contract. Not having a contract could lead to trouble down the road, especially if a problem crops up in the renovation. Write up a contract and ensure both you and your renovator sign it to ensure responsibilities are met.

9

Becoming a
Landlord

---

*Y*our partner finally popped the question, or maybe it was you who did the asking, and now the two of you plan to buy a house. Or, you just got offered a job overseas and there is no way you will pass up the opportunity. But you own a home. Should you sell it or rent it out?

The answer depends on your goals. It may also depend on how much you can get if you sell the home. If you have the aptitude and the stamina to be a landlord, you might be best to rent your home, use the income to pay the mortgage and taxes (plus a little extra for your trouble), and let the property appreciate.

Natalie, the Toronto journalist, says she will rent out her condo if a live-in relationship comes along in her future. She says keeping her condo is like having "relationship insurance." "If and when I decide to get into a relationship where we share accommodation, I would keep the property and use it as a financial investment," says Natalie. "It's also a type of insurance because, if something happened to the relationship, I would still have something I went into the relationship with—a roof over my head that's mine."

Breanne, a twenty-something nurse from Hamilton, Ontario, bristles at the suggestion. "That is a hard situation, because you are setting up the relationship or marriage for failure." Instead, Breanne says she would likely sell her place if she were to get married.

To each her own.

If you think you'd be likely to sell if Mr. Right came along, Chapter Ten is for you.

If you plan to rent the home, there is a lot of information you must have before becoming a landlord. In this chapter you will find out what you need to know, whether you are renting a room or an apartment in your own home to help pay the bills or you have an investment rental property.

Being a landlord can be a lot of work, but it can also be financially rewarding.

Second Suites (also known as "Granny Flats")

Kathy, the fifty-something City of Toronto employee, bought her home more than 15 years ago, when she was in her late thirties. The three-bedroom house is in Toronto's west end, near Humber College and not far from Pearson International Airport. As a single woman on a government salary, Kathy found herself a bit stretched financially at first, but she wanted a big home that she could grow into over the years.

"I wanted a place I could settle into for the duration. I always say my next home will be the funeral home," Kathy says, laughing. Her plan was to rent out two of the bedrooms to local college students for a few years, until she was able to manage the mortgage payments on her own. But after a while, Kathy found having the college students in her home "too intrusive."

What she really wanted were tenants she didn't have to spend so much time with. Ideally, she wanted tenants who didn't live there. While it sounds like an impossible scenario, Kathy found a brilliant solution. "I rent to airline pilots," says Kathy, whose home is a short commute from the airport. "I had an air traffic controller from the United States rent a room at my house for about five years. My current tenant lives in Calgary, but flies in and out of Hamilton a lot," Kathy says.

What's more, she has made a lot of friends in foreign cities this way. On some occasions, Kathy will even cook for the weary shift workers, many of whom haven't had a home-cooked meal in months. While she no longer needs to rent the rooms to keep up the mortgage, Kathy says she uses the extra money for vacations. She also enjoys the company from time to time.

"People often ask me, 'Don't you miss the privacy?' but I have organized it so that I do have a lot of private time," Kathy says. She asks her tenants to give her their schedules in advance and sometimes, when she knows they will be staying a full weekend, she goes out of town on a mini-vacation of her own. "I would tell any single woman to rent out rooms to anyone who works long or intense hours, such as doctors, firefighters or pilots," Kathy says.

Beth in Newfoundland wasn't as lucky with her live-in roommate. She rented out a room not just to help pay the mortgage, but because she was nervous about living on her own in such a big house. She started asking friends if they knew anyone who needed to rent a room. As it turned out, a former roommate from her tenant days was looking, and moved in about a week after Beth took possession of her house.

While she felt safe, and was able to make the mortgage payments easily for the first several months, Beth didn't foresee how different the living arrangement would be once she became the landlord rather than a roommate. "It was a terrible experience," Beth recalls. "When it's your own home, you really feel like there is an interloper in your space."

Beth says her mistake was not laying out the ground rules from the start. "I wasn't clear enough about my expectations, about what someone living in my house should do. You have to differentiate between the personal and the business. Women are socialized to 'make nice' all the time. So I didn't say anything about what was bothering me for the longest time."

Finally, Beth told her roommate she could handle the expenses on her own, and requested she move out. In hindsight, Beth says she probably could have carried the expenses and saved herself the stress of an uncomfortable living arrangement.

If you decide to rent a suite in your home (also known as a granny flat, accessory apartment or in-law suite), you should review your town or city bylaws. There are different rules for renting a room in your home, and renting out an apartment with its own entrance, kitchen and bathroom.

Most bylaws encourage second suites because it creates more affordable housing. That said, your suite may not be "legal" according to municipal bylaws. The benefits of legalizing your second suite are to reduce your liability. This means ensuring your suite meets all required fire, building and housing standards and is accounted for in both your insurance policy and mortgage agreement. Of course, some people set up illegal rental suites because they want to avoid the "hassles" of meeting all those regulations, but in doing so they are leaving themselves open to liability, fines, insurance problems, etc.

If you do decide to put a second suite in your home, consider the ramifications for your lifestyle. Yes, you will get extra income, but you will also pay extra money to maintain the suite. You also have legal obligations to consider. As a landlord—and this goes for all rental scenarios—you have rights and responsibilities, and so does your tenant. You'll need to do some research before entering into a landlord-tenant agreement.

Landlord and tenant legislation is different in every province and territory. For example, you cannot collect a security deposit in Ontario or Quebec. In Alberta, unless there is an agreement in writing, interest on the security deposit is paid annually. Keep in mind that laws can and do change, so ensure you have the most up-to-date legislation for both landlords and tenants—and make sure you look at both provincial and municipal laws. You need all the facts when you're dealing with rent increases, for example, damage to your property, or how to end the landlord-tenant agreement.

You should also be aware that there are new privacy laws in Canada that may impact what information you can collect from a prospective tenant. Under the new legislation, you need to tell the tenants why you are collecting the information and what you plan to do with it. More information on the new privacy laws can be found at the Privacy Commissioner's website at: http://www.privcom.gc.ca/ekit/index_e.asp.

Obtaining legal advice may also be wise, but make sure the lawyer deals specifically in this specialized area. Stanleigh Palka, a lawyer who specializes in landlord-tenant law, civil litigation and family law with Lancaster, Brooks & Welch LLP in St. Catharines, Ontario, says too many people become landlords because they believe it's an easy way to make money.

"Think again," says Stanleigh. "Delving into residential rental properties can be a very profitable enterprise, but you must operate within a complex network of strict regulations, rules, and laws that do not always work in your favour."

Stanleigh says you should not enter the landlord-tenant agreement with the view that renters are deadbeats (after all, you were a renter once, weren't you?). "Most tenants are good, honest people who want to establish and maintain a positive, mutually beneficial relationship with their landlord," he says. "Don't let tales of a few rotten apples spoil it for the rest of the bunch. But just be ready when one of those rotten apples ends up in your rental property."

Although most tenants work hard and obey laws, he says there are a few who show no regard for the law or other people's property. Stanleigh says it's your job as the landlord to be responsible, not only for the sake of your property, but for your renters too. "You owe it to yourself and your honest tenants to keep your rental property clean and safe."

For more information on landlord and tenant situations, I asked Stanleigh Palka a few questions. (Please note: all answers assume that the landlord and tenant are situated in Ontario. Each province in Canada has its own landlord-tenant legislation.)

1. Can you give some advice on the right way to find a tenant?

Always ask for references from former landlords—and then follow up with those former landlords. Many landlords ask for references, then do nothing with them. If possible, meet with the prospective tenants face to face. Sometimes that is impractical because a family may be relocating from the other side of the country and they cannot meet with the landlord before the permanent move. A telephone call is the next best option. Of course, the Ontario Human Rights Code (OHRC) prohibits discrimination when selecting a tenant based on 16 grounds. A landlord cannot turn down a prospective tenant on any of the grounds enumerated in the OHRC, including but not limited to race, religion, age, disabilities or sexual orientation.

If a prospective tenant smokes or has pets, a landlord can refuse to rent. This is because the Ontario Rental Housing Tribunal (ORHT) does not cover individuals before they become tenants. If these issues are important to the landlord, he or she should ask about them before renting to the person. Once the person is a tenant, evicting because he or she smokes or has a pet tends to be difficult and only ordered where it can be shown by the landlord that the smoking or pets are causing damage to the property or bothering other tenants.

2. Is it necessary to have a lease?

Although a written rental agreement (i.e., a lease) is not required under the Tenant Protection Act, I would recommend one. Having a lease helps to avoid any confusion concerning the rights and obligations of the landlord and the tenant. A properly drafted lease will set out, among other things, such terms as rent, when the rent is due, who has the responsibility to pay utilities, and the allowable uses of the rental unit.

3. What are your rights as a landlord when it comes to taking back the property from the tenant?

Broadly speaking, a landlord can evict a tenant based on two grounds: 1) cause and 2) non-cause. Cause grounds mean that the tenant did something wrong. However, that "something wrong," that activity, must affect the nature of the rental unit in order to evict. For example, if a tenant is convicted of drug trafficking, but the criminal activity did not occur in or around the rental unit, the Ontario Rental Housing Tribunal (ORHT) may not order an eviction. Non-cause grounds for eviction are used when the tenant has done nothing wrong per se, but the landlord requires vacant possession of the rental unit. For example, the landlord may need the rental unit for his or her own personal use or may wish to convert the rental unit to commercial use.

continued

4. What is the correct way to get rid of a tenant who is causing problems, or whom other tenants are complaining about?

The Tenant Protection Act strictly regulates how a landlord can deal with troublesome tenants. One of the biggest misconceptions of uninitiated landlords is to believe that they can simply knock on the door of the rental unit and demand that the tenant vacate immediately.

Regardless of how egregiously a tenant may be acting, a landlord must follow the proper process in seeking an eviction. In the case of a tenant who falls behind on rent, the landlord will start by serving a written notice to terminate the tenancy on grounds of non-payment of rent. The landlord can obtain the form for such a notice from the Ontario Rental Housing Tribunal. The tenant has 14 days to pay the rent owed after receiving the notice of termination.

If the tenant pays, the process ends and the tenant remains. If the tenant does not pay, the landlord can apply to the ORHT to terminate the tenancy on the fourteenth day. Typically, the case will be heard at the tribunal within one month and the resulting order is released about one week after the hearing.

The tribunal supplies a trained mediator who, with the consent of the landlord and tenant, will discuss the issues and recommend a settlement. The recommendation is non-binding on the parties and either party can stop the mediation at any point for whatever reason.

Practically speaking, except in extreme circumstances, it is advisable that the landlord try to talk about the problems with the tenant.

Often, tenants do not realize that their loud music, for instance, is disturbing neighbouring tenants. Once advised, those tenants might correct their offending behaviour. If not, the landlord should consider pursuing an eviction at that point or risk losing good tenants who cannot tolerate the troublesome tenant any longer.

On another practical note, a landlord should not wait until the tenant is many months behind on rent before issuing a notice of termination. Landlords should take steps to enforce their rights to collect full rent on a timely basis, without delay. Most tenants cannot afford to pay thousands of dollars in back rent at once to bring the rent into good standing. Faced with the prospect of eviction, some tenants will gather their belongings and surreptitiously sneak out of the rental unit without leaving a forwarding address or any other information with the landlord. The landlord is left with an empty rental unit, large rental arrears, and little hope of recovering those funds.

5. What are some of the common mistakes landlords make when it comes to taking on tenants?

The most common mistake that landlords make when taking on a tenant is assuming that they can remove a tenant swiftly and without much effort or expense, for whatever reason and whenever they want. Many landlords fail to understand just how regulated this area has become.

In Ontario, residential landlord-tenant relations are governed by a far-reaching web of laws, regulations and rules that arguably favour tenants. The law was crafted on the assumption that an inherent power imbalance exists between landlords and tenants. On the one hand, landlords have the resources to hold rental property, whereas, on the other hand, tenants typically are renting because they cannot qualify for or maintain even a modest mortgage on a home.

6. Not all tenants have bad intentions, correct? After all, most of us have been renters at some point in our lives!

The vast majority of tenants are honest, law-abiding citizens who want nothing more than to establish a home, even if it is temporary, and a strong, positive relationship with their landlord. In my practice, I hear the tales of disaster. Just as the plane that lands smoothly doesn't make the evening news report, I don't have landlords walking

continued

into my office telling me about the tenant they have had for over 10 years and with whom they exchange Christmas gifts. I have to deal with the landlord whose tenant is running a prostitution and cocaine ring out of their rental unit, harassing the other good tenants, and threatening to burn down the apartment if the landlord looks at them the wrong way. Obviously, that is a worst-case scenario.

More often, I provide representation to the landlord who has issues with an otherwise good tenant who is two or three months behind on rent

Finding the Perfect Tenant

Finding a good tenant includes more than just a gut feeling that the person is trustworthy to live in your home. You have to advertise in the right places, ask a fair price, and check out the person's references and credit history.

When Jennifer, the event producer you've come to know well in these pages, moved in with her boyfriend (now husband), she decided to rent out her loft instead of selling it. At first she rented it to a friend who had just moved to Toronto and was saving money to buy her own condo. When she moved out a few months later, Jennifer had no choice but to rent to strangers for the first time, which gave her a much different feeling than renting to a friend. "It was very hard for me to let go, to have people in there I didn't know," Jennifer recalls. "You just cross your fingers and hope they don't destroy the place."

Jennifer set out some criteria before starting her search. She wanted a non-smoker and a tenant(s) who would care enough about the place to decorate in a tasteful way. She also wanted to ensure the tenant was a professional and financially responsible. She put an ad in the newspaper. The day after it ran, Jennifer received a dozen calls from interested tenants. She held an open house, and in the end chose a couple that met her criteria, and with whom she felt she could easily communicate. Her tenants turned out to be reasonable, and only called with a few complaints—all of which Jennifer was easily able to handle.

Karen, the twenty-something Burford, Ontario, school teacher, rented out her rural home after landing a job in Scotland for a year. At first, she didn't think she could take a year off, but then concluded that owning a home shouldn't hold her back. "Taking a trip is 'doable.' You have to be the kind of person who can let go. I am surprised at myself that I did, because I didn't think I was the type that could. The key is to find someone to rent the place that you feel you can trust. There are no guarantees, but I wasn't going to give up the opportunity based on what-if," Karen says.

Karen's home is large and fully furnished, and she didn't want the hassle of moving her stuff out for the year. That meant finding a tenant she could trust not only living in her home, but using her furniture and other belongings as well. "I found someone that I knew, but wasn't too close with, so I could make the arrangement businesslike as well," Karen says. With the help of a friend's mother, who is a lawyer, Karen drew up a rental agreement that she and the tenant signed. It included responsibility for the home and furnishings, but also for the utility bills, which remained in Karen's name. "I figure it helped both of us save money: she didn't have to pay for connection fees when she moved in and I didn't have to pay for them when I returned."

Karen did notice some wear and tear left by her tenant during that year she was away, but says that should be expected by any landlord. "You have to expect a bit of damage. There might be a few nicks and scratches here and there, but then again, who knows what damage I may have caused on my own if I had been there!"

Finding good tenants takes strategy. Try to think of the last time you rented, how you found the apartment and what you liked, or disliked, about the landlord and the rental agreement. Where you market the property is important. Jennifer chose a newspaper whose typical reader profile matched the kind of tenant she was looking for. Other avenues, depending on where you live, include signage and postings through online classified services (such as Craigslist), which have become very popular in recent years. If you have the technology, providing digital photos of the apartment and posting them online is a great way to advertise the rental unit. It can save time because it eliminates the first stage in the selection process, since only those who like what they see in the images will ask to check out the place in person.

In a renter's market (that is, when there are more available spaces than tenants to fill them), you may have to market your property more. You might consider offering incentives such as free utilities and cable, and maybe even a break on the rent. You may need to be flexible. It's better to have a tenant who pays a little less rent than you are asking than having no tenant at all. For instance, if you are asking $1,200 a month (that's $14,400 a year), but your potential tenants say they can afford only $1,150 a month ($13,800 a year), you might be better off accepting their offer than leaving the apartment vacant for a month, or more. The $50 difference per month works out to $600 a year, compared to the $1200 you would lose each month the place wasn't rented. When it comes to pricing your property, do your own search, as though you were a potential renter in today's market, and find out what's fair remuneration for the space you are renting.

Choosing a Tenant

Once you have your prospective tenant, you will want to check their history. For starters, get them to fill out a rental application. You can get sample forms from your local housing office or try the Canada Mortgage and Housing Corporation website:

http://www.cmhc.ca/en/co/reho/yogureho/salewo/salewo_014.
cfm?renderforprint=1

Rental applications include personal information such as name, address and telephone numbers, employment information, banking information and references. If you rent to anyone without having all this information, you may find it difficult to terminate the rental agreement should problems arise down the road. I've already pointed out how important it is to actually check the references once you have the necessary information in hand, but you might still be wondering what I mean. Here's a detailed list of what and how to check:

- Check the applicant's banking history and/or credit bureau history. Privacy laws mean you will not be able to get banking information from a bank or other lender without the written permission of the applicant. A quicker step may be to call a credit bureau to check the information. A fee will apply.
- Confirm the applicant's employment situation by calling the employer they've listed.
- Check the applicant's tenancy history/evictions, if available. This means getting names and numbers of previous landlords (as many as two or three) and calling them for more information.
- Check court records, if available. Court records are, for the most part, public record. You can head down to a local courthouse and do a check, or hire a lawyer to do the execution search for you. That said, you would have to know which areas to search since court checks do not cover all jurisdictions in Canada (or other countries).
- Call anyone else the applicant has listed as a reference, unless it is a family member of the applicant and therefore not a reliable source of information.

There are basic questions you should ask a prospective tenant, but there are also questions that, by law, you cannot ask as a potential landlord.

As a landlord you can ask:

- Where do you work? What is your income?

- How many people will be living with you and what are their names?

- Do you have pets? Do you smoke?

- Could you provide written permission for a credit check?

- May I see your references and their current contact information?

As a landlord you cannot ask:

- Do you plan to have (more) children?

- What is your ethnic background, religion or sexual preference?

- Will your family be visiting?

- What is your social insurance number? (The applicant may voluntarily provide a SIN, but you cannot refuse to rent to someone on the basis of not providing a SIN.)

- Are you married, single or divorced?

Remember that while you want to get as much information as possible about the prospective tenant, there are provincial laws that prohibit you from choosing a tenant based on factors such as ancestry, place of origin, colour, ethnic origin, citizenship, creed, sex, age, marital status, family status, handicap or the receipt of public assistance. You cannot refuse to rent an apartment based on these characteristics.

Once you've chosen the tenant you want, and you've come to an agreement together about the tenancy details, you should collect first and last month's rent, or a deposit, depending on which province you live in.

Before You Add Landlord to Your List of Titles...

Even before you go searching for just the right tenant, you'll need to familiarize yourself with the various responsibilities that you'll be taking on as a landlord. It's your job to ensure the property meets all laws and regulations, from zoning to fire safety to building codes, and that it stays that way at all times.

Here's another handy list from CMHC on the most basic responsibilities of each party in a tenancy agreement.

Landlords must:

- Maintain the tenant's home in a good state of repair and fit for habitation and at the landlord's expense comply with health, safety, housing and maintenance standards.

- Not withhold, during a tenant's occupancy, the reasonable supply of fuel, electricity, hot and cold water and other utility services (cable, Internet) unless the tenant has agreed to obtain and pay for these services.

- Not interfere with the reasonable enjoyment of the tenant and the members of his or her household and guests.

- Not seize, without legal process, a tenant's property for rent default or for the breach of any other obligation of the tenant.

- Not harass, obstruct, coerce, threaten or interfere with the tenant.

Tenants must:

- Pay the rent on time.

- Behave well, clean the rental premises, repair damage caused by any willful or negligent act of the tenant or a person whom the tenant permits on the premises.

- Not harass, obstruct, coerce, threaten or interfere with the landlord.

- Contact the landlord as soon as possible when a serious problem arises involving repairs or services.

- Permit entry (with proper notice) for repairs or showing of premises for next tenant or purchaser.

(Source: Canada Mortgage and Housing Corporation)

As a landlord, you are responsible for many things. There is an important difference, though, between attending to emergencies and making necessary repairs. While you want to maintain the property, not everything has to be done immediately, even if the tenant requests that it be fixed. An emergency repair is one that impacts the health and safety of the tenant or puts the property at risk. It's the landlord's responsibility, by law, to handle and pay for such repairs.

That said, there are non-emergency repairs that require your attention but are more of an inconvenience than an emergency. Here are some examples of both scenarios.

Emergency repairs include:

✓ Broken pipe(s) that are flooding the premises.

✓ The heating system is not functioning when it is cold outside.

✓ The sewage system is backing up into the premises.

✓ A defective lock lets anyone gain entry to the premises without a key.

✓ A short circuit in the wiring is creating a risk of fire and/or electrocution.

✓ The refrigerator supplied by the landlord is not working.

Non-emergency repairs include:

✓ An interior door doesn't close properly.

✓ A stove element is burnt out.

✓ The kitchen sink drains slowly.

✓ There is a minor leak in the roof.

✓ There is a minor leak or dripping in household plumbing.

✓ A garage door opener is not working, but manual access is still available.

✓ There is a cracked pane in an upper window.

(Source: Canada Mortgage and Housing Corporation)

What to Do About Problem Tenants

Fixing problems with your property is one headache you have to deal with as a landlord. Another is problem tenants. Tenants who don't pay rent, make too much noise or damage the property are potential problems you need to be prepared for if you plan to be a landlord.

Noise complaints can often be handled by talking to the tenant directly, or calling the police if the problem persists.

Responsibility for damage is something that should be laid out in the rental agreement. You may want to protect yourself by including a clause that states a tenant is responsible for any major damage done to your property. Remember, though, as Karen said earlier, some wear and tear should be expected.

If the tenant doesn't pay the rent on time, you need to decide if you want to keep nagging, or have the tenant move out. If you want them to move, a notice of non-payment is required. In most provinces, the notice can be given within the first three days of non-payment of rent. According to CMHC, a notice of non-payment includes the amount of rent that the tenant owes, the date by which the tenant is to move out, and a statement that says the tenant can disagree with the landlord's notice.

If the tenant doesn't budge, you can get help from the provincial rental authority to order the tenant to move. If this is the route you have to take, remember to play by the rules, and keep records. This can turn into a legal battle, and if it does you want to ensure that you have your argument in good order.

Kathryn, the fifty-something market research consultant who told you about her renovating experience in Chapter Eight, dabbled in the role of landlord. She bought two investment properties in Toronto, both with multiple tenants. One was a triplex in the Yonge and Sheppard area, in the north end of Toronto, while the second was near Christie and St. Clair Avenue, in the city's central-west end.

"It was difficult," Kathryn recalls of the experience. Not only did she assume the landlord lifestyle during a renter's market (vacancy rates were high), but she inherited some problem tenants when she purchased the homes. Her first bad experience was with a tenant who turned out to be a drug addict and couldn't pay the rent. Kathryn had to go to his parents to get the money. What's more, the tenant was loud, which drew complaints from the other renters in the building.

She also rented a basement apartment to two young women who were living without their parents' supervision for the first time. They threw loud parties, and allowed a third tenant to camp out in the home for weeks. The last straw was when they left a sofa on the front lawn because they couldn't fit it in the apartment.

Then there was the tenant who left the windows open all day, at the same time the air conditioner was on full blast. The electricity costs were included in the rent, so Kathryn was paying for this illogical extravagance.

"It's very hard to get rid of a tenant for anything except non-payment," Kathryn says. "Of the eight renters I had, I would only have considered renting to two of them. Most of them didn't care about the property." Kathryn found herself frustrated by the complaints, especially from the tenants she respected. "I couldn't stand the phone calls because I wanted to do something. Some people can let stuff like that roll off their backs—not me. There would be complaints about noise, or other things. I felt terrible unless I could do something about it."

After a couple of years, Kathryn decided the landlord life was not for her. She eventually sold both properties. "It was supposed to be part of my retirement income, but I guess I'll just get the money from somewhere else."

Dealing with tenants can be tough, as you can see from Kathryn's situation. That said, a lot of single women have stuck it out with success.

The Vacancy Issue

One last thing to be prepared for as a landlord is having your apartment sit vacant. The risk, like any investment, is losing money for that month (or months) when the unit sits vacant.

Jennifer, the marketing manager we met in Chapter Three, says she had a perfect tenant when she was a landlord. Jennifer moved out of her condo after buying a larger place in the same building. Instead of selling the unit, she tried renting it. Her first experience as a landlord was positive. "My tenant was perfect. If she had a leak in the place, she would fix it herself. It was quite a good situation."

It was after the tenant moved out that Jennifer had problems. She hired a real estate agent to help her find a new tenant, but after three months, and a huge bill from the agent, the unit was still empty. Jennifer decided to sell, and give up the hassle of trying to find tenants.

"Being a landlord is not a sure thing," says Erica, the twenty-something journalism student who has a condo in downtown Toronto. Before moving out west in 2005, Erica's place sat empty for months while she hired decorators to prepare the place for a new tenant. Her problem was not so much finding a suitable tenant, but leaving the renovation work to others while she was away.

"If you cannot be the person looking after your own place, finding someone to get it done, and quickly, can be a problem. Every month someone isn't in there costs you. And nobody cares as much about your property as you do."

Toronto realtor Brad Lamb believes the biggest problem many single women have to overcome when it comes to being a landlord is losing the "nice girl" image. "This is another wide-sweeping statement," he says, "but I find women are generally nicer people than men. Not many women have started wars, and there aren't many female mass murderers. That said, you cannot really be nice as a landlord. You have to say, 'Pay the rent, or I'm kicking you out.'" He adds that you don't have to be "super smart" to be a landlord, but you do have to be super prepared.

Checklist: If You're Going to Be a Landlord

✓ Learn about the laws that govern the landlord-tenant relationship in your area.

✓ Make sure the property you're renting meets all building safety and zoning requirements.

✓ Advertise the space and set a reasonable price for it.

✓ Check references of prospective tenants, and run credit bureau checks.

✓ Know the difference between emergency and non-emergency calls from your tenant. In emergencies, act immediately.

✓ Be financially prepared. You'll need back-up money to pay the mortgage and utilities if a tenant moves out and the apartment sits vacant for a month or more.

Common Mistakes to Avoid:

✗ Overcharging for rent. Finding tenants will be hard, or you may lose them to more reasonably priced apartments.

✗ Not checking references. Having a gut feeling that a person is able to pay the rent is not enough. Check their references, including employers and past landlords, and do a credit check.

✗ Not fixing problems in a timely way. If the rental unit's roof is leaking or the basement is flooded, act. You need to look after the needs of your home and the people who are paying you to live there. Be respectful.

10

Is It Time to *Sell?*

---

*S*ome relationships just aren't meant to last forever. It may have been love at first sight, but deep down you knew the time would come when you would be ready to move on.

Selling your home can be stressful, but you can make the parting of ways go smoothly. You need to detach your emotions and see it for what it is—a business deal. And just think: if circumstances are good you can probably make some money in this transaction. See—breaking up isn't so hard to do after all!

To Be, or Not to Be, Your Own Agent

The first thing you have to decide is whether you will use an agent or try to sell the home privately.

When I sold my loft in downtown Toronto, I tried to do a private sale first. My building had 11 units, all different shapes and sizes, and an eclectic group of tenants. I put notices under their doors, assuming that if they had friends or family who liked their lofts, they might be interested in buying mine. One person did look seriously at the space—a friend of the woman who lived above me—but he decided the price I was asking was too high. He turned out to be right.

While I was sure my loft would sell in the low $300,000 range, it actually sold four months later, after I'd used a real estate agent and dropped the price twice, for $285,000. I still made a little bit of money, having lived there for two years, but I also learned that no matter how great I thought my space was, the market would determine its real worth.

"You are always going to think your property is worth more because it's your personal space," advises Esther, whom you've met in previous chapters.

Using an agent means paying a real estate commission on the sale of the home, which can range anywhere from 4 to 6 percent, or more, depending on the property. You can try to negotiate with the agent to lower the fee, but no matter how low you go you will be paying a significant sum. Private selling allows you to bypass the sales commission altogether, which is the great attraction of it.

If you sell on your own you can save money, but your property may not get the number of "eyeballs" it would if you listed it through an agent. An agent can advertise your home through the Multiple Listing Service, a product of the Canadian Real Estate Association that gives other agents access to your information as they're searching on behalf of their clients—no matter where those clients may be. That service is where the great majority of homes for sale in Canada are listed. When you list with an agent, your home will be posted on the MLS website (mls.ca), and will probably be advertised in newspapers and other places where potential buyers look for their next home. Remember how you found your home to begin with? It's the same process, in reverse. Keep this in mind through all the stages of selling your home.

I've seen a number of homeowners try to sell their homes on their own, holding open houses and posting signs. Most of them, within a week or two, wind up with a real estate agent's sign on their lawn, and their house is sold soon after.

That said, more people are selling on their own, especially with the help of the Internet. When you sell your home on your own, the listing is known in the industry as "For Sale By Owner," or FSBO for short. This means you are acting as your own agent. These listings include everything from a handmade sign on the front lawn, to newspapers listings, to websites designed for FSBO sales.

If you take this route, remember the process may be slower than if you were to use an agent who has access to the Multiple Listing Service. If you are determined to sell on your own, you can also advertise your home in newspapers, magazines or by simply putting up signs in your neighbourhood. Try to advertise in publications or places that might appeal to potential buyers.

Below is a list of home-selling considerations.

As your own agent, you will have to:

- determine the market price of your home
- design the marketing plan
- prepare, schedule, run and pay for your ads
- screen inquiries
- screen potential buyers by asking the right questions

- book appointments
- be available to show your home
- be familiar with the legalities of an offer (hiring a lawyer is recommended)
- negotiate the offer and counter-offers
- collect and coordinate all legal documentation

If you hire a real estate agent, he or she should:

- draw up the "listing agreement," your formal contract with the real estate brokerage firm
- explain the home-selling process to you in detail
- provide you with a comprehensive market analysis that compares your home with similar properties recently sold in your area (individual features, condition, asking and selling prices)
- provide advice on enhancing your home's sales appeal
- design and implement a marketing plan (including an advertising schedule) to promote your home
- screen and pre-qualify potential buyers, schedule appointments and bring buyers through
- negotiate the offer to purchase on your behalf and present your counter-offers to the buyer
- generally advise you of legal and financial responsibilities
- assist you in completing the sale

(Source: Royal Bank of Canada)

In the end, you should choose the selling method that makes you feel most comfortable. As you can see from the list above, selling on your own is a lot of responsibility, not to mention a time and energy commitment. If you are up for it, and you have time to sell, you may wish to try doing it on your own. However, if you have to sell quickly because you are moving, or you've bought a new place with a closing date that's fast approaching, it could be worth the commission you'll pay to have an agent facilitate the sale.

If you use an agent, and had a good experience with the one who sold you the home, go back to them. If not, choose a selling agent using much of the same advice given in Chapter Two. You want to work with someone who has your best interests in mind.

Regardless of whether you are using an agent, or acting on your own to sell your home, there are a lot of factors to consider before putting up that for-sale sign. We'll go through them all, starting with what price to ask.

The Price Is Right

Setting the right price for your home is crucial.

If your asking price is too high, you reduce the number of interested buyers. Many real estate experts recommend pricing a home at 5 or 10 percent above market value. By doing so, you are more likely to receive an offer closer to the true value of your home. Remember, it's the real estate market that dictates what your home is worth, not you.

Overpricing your home is a turnoff to potential buyers and could mean your home sits on the market for a longer period of time. In a steady housing market, buyers may wonder if something is wrong with the home if it hasn't sold in a few weeks. This is especially true in large cities. Rural listings may be more of an exception.

Angela Nolan, the Hamilton real estate agent and former single homeowner, says she can usually predict within $5,000 how much a home will sell for in her area. "Pricing a house properly at first is very important," Angela advises her clients. "A house that is priced properly is two-thirds sold."

One advantage to using an agent when selling your home is that he or she can help you determine what price you should list it for. Agents do this by searching a database for recent home sales in your area. They compare the features of those homes to the features of yours, and help you determine a reasonable price for your home.

If you want a completely objective opinion, you can also hire an appraiser to assess your home's value. He or she will also use recent home sales in your area to determine a fair market price. The difference is that an appraiser has no vested interest in suggesting either a high or low price—they charge a set fee rather than receiving a percentage of your home's selling price, as an agent will do.

You also may wish to bring back the home inspector you used when you first bought the place. The inspector can reassess the house and tell you if there are any major problems. For instance, if the roof needs fixing, you may wish to do it before you sell the home. Listing a home with a new roof will likely attract a higher price. That's because the potential buyer will do his/her own inspection after the two of you have negotiated a price. If the buyer finds the roof needs fixing, you may be forced to drop the price significantly to cover the costs, or face the possibility that the buyer walks away from the deal. You want to eliminate any surprises a potential buyer may come across when looking through your home.

You can also present the results of the home inspection to potential buyers—it will show that you have nothing to hide. But even if you have another home inspection done, don't be surprised if a potential buyer hires their own firm to inspect the property separately. You have to understand their wanting to get a second opinion. What's more, in their shoes, you would probably do the same.

Make a Good First Impression

Would you buy a new white blouse if it had a coffee stain on it? How about a car with an interior that smelled like a wet dog? House shopping is not much different from shopping for other products. Remember that your potential buyer needs to like what they see. This means presenting your home at its best.

It helps to think of selling your home as entering it in a beauty contest. You are competing against dozens of other contenders with their own beautiful qualities. Your goal is to win this pageant by putting your home's best face forward.

So what does that mean? You've probably heard the tricks: the smell of baked bread, light music in the background, lots of light. It's true that all of these really can help when presenting your home to potential buyers. And, if you have watched any of the reality TV shows about how to get a higher price for your home, you'll know about the importance of clearing away junk. Cleaning and de-cluttering your home really is key. Potential buyers of your home don't want to see your collection of matches from all the bars you've been to across the country, the dozens of overpriced face creams and cleansers that litter your bathroom counter, or the *Cosmo* magazines that clutter your coffee table.

Before you let potential buyers into your home, the space should look like a hotel. You want those buyers to feel comfortable, not as if they're intruding on your personal space (even though they are—but you want that!).

Remember, too, that your home must be appealing to both men and women buyers. A 2006 poll of potential buyers showed 41 percent of men said they were more likely to put a premium on decor, compared to 31 percent of women. The 2006 Royal LePage House Staging Poll (conducted by Maritz Research) also showed that renovations can increase the value of a home, but too much of a unique style can be a turnoff.

"First impressions are key in real estate, since buyers often make up their minds about a home within the first few minutes of entering the front door," says Dianne Usher, a vice-president with Royal LePage Real Estate Services. "As the real estate market begins to moderate in many markets across the country, the need to impress buyers becomes even more crucial. A combination of the right renovations with modern and tasteful decor is the best way to do that." Diane adds, "A contemporary and minimalist space, with neutral-coloured walls and a limited number of personal items, appeals to most buyers and ensures the best results when selling a home."

The Royal LePage survey also found the following percentage of buyers would pay a premium for certain features.

- Renovated kitchen: 79 percent
- Renovated bathroom: 73 percent
- New windows: 70 percent
- New flooring: 62 percent
- Updated decor: 36 percent

In addition, while 47 percent of buyers said that the need for major renovations would most negatively influence their buying decision, a significant proportion of buyers (11 percent) thought that decor requiring major changes had the most impact on their decision. Only 6 percent of buyers said that the need for minor renovations would most negatively influence their buying decision.

"The way you live in your home is not the way you sell your home. If you are renovating primarily to increase the value of your home for a sale, you need to ensure that it is done in a style that is pleasing to most buyers," Timothy Badgley, interior designer and owner of Acanthus Interiors in Port Hope, Ontario, said of the survey results. "Not all renovations are created equal. Style and decor are especially important with large renovations, as these features will be costly to change for a buyer and they can be a major factor in buying decisions."

The poll also found:

- Sixty-three percent of buyers preferred a higher priced home that does not require any renovations over a lower priced fixer-upper.
- Fifty-eight percent of buyers revealed that they were willing to make a decision after viewing 10 homes or fewer, while only 11 percent of buyers thought they would have to view more than 20 homes in order to feel comfortable making a decision.
- An overwhelming majority of people (83 percent) surveyed said that they would regard their realtor's assessment of the home as somewhat or very important. As such, sellers need to impress both potential buyers and realtors, who are local market experts. This dynamic raises the bar for anyone wanting to sell a home.
- When asked which room of the house had the most significant impact on their purchasing decision, 52 percent of buyers said the kitchen and 25 percent said the living room. A surprisingly low 5 percent of buyers thought the bathroom had the greatest impact.

The Canada Mortgage and Housing Corporation puts it well when they say: "Potential buyers are not interested in hearing about your good intentions to look after defects before a transfer of ownership take place. Even if fix-up work is underway, buyers may not be able to visualize what your home will look like when the work is finished. They will just remember it being in a state of disrepair."

The Five Senses of Home Selling

When it comes to primping your home for showings to potential buyers, think of the five senses: sight, hearing, taste, touch and smell. When someone walks through the front door of your home, all their senses should feel pleased. Let's go through what I call the five senses of home selling.

Sight

First impressions are everything. A prospective buyer will be trying to picture themselves in your space. This is what you want. Now is the time to be like that Type A roommate you had in college. Think Monica on the hit TV show *Friends*. Again, think beauty pageant. Your home is on display.

For starters, make sure it's clean, top to bottom. This includes removing dirty dishes from the sink, putting away your dirty boots and shoes, and finally organizing the closets like you promised yourself you would do years ago.

A fresh coat of paint where needed can also do a lot to increase a room's visual appeal. Neutral colours are best because they are appealing to a greater number of people. That dusty rose colour in the living room may be nice to you, but not everyone will agree.

Now, let the light shine in! This is important when it comes to showing your home. Even the smallest room looks larger with the curtains open and sun shining in. Of course, don't forget to clean the windows. The sunshine is great, but not if it highlights the dirt and streaks on your windows.

If your home is filled with memorabilia, such as that shrine to Madonna, or photos of you and friends with Chippendales dancers, put it away. Potential buyers want to imagine themselves living in your home, not try to figure out what kind of adult still worships the Material Girl.

Make sure minor flaws are fixed. This includes everything from fixing dripping taps and replacing burnt-out light bulbs to tightening loose, creaky floorboards. Make sure the doors, windows and closets open and close properly. Anything that creaks need to be fixed—creaks are for horror films, not homes trying to sell for top dollar.

Finally, keep furniture to a minimum. This allows rooms to look larger and ensures easier movement as people view your home. If you have too much stuff, consider storing some of it until the house is sold.

Hearing

Turn off the TV, radio and dishwasher and stop talking on the phone. What do you hear? Is the garage band next door too loud? How about the neighbour's dog (or yours), or the sound of traffic from the highway?

These sounds are what potential home buyers will hear when they come through your home. I once lost a potential buyer when selling my Toronto loft after a friend staying in one of the units near me decided to play the drums at the time of the showing. I later reasoned with the wannabe rock star that he should practise elsewhere. He was happy to oblige.

While some noise can be expected, remember that you are trying to please the senses. Close any windows that are likely to let in the most offensive sounds, such as highway traffic. It's not a bad idea to put on some soft music in the background. (Your favourite heavy metal station is not recommended.) Think of the music you hear when you enter a spa or fine dining restaurant. Think relaxing sounds, and play them for your guests as they snoop around your home.

Taste

This is not a suggestion that you feed your guests. They are there to snack on your personal space, not on those oatmeal cookies you burned the night before. When it comes to home selling, taste has to do with the style of your home.

This is where the neutral paint comes in, as well as the removal of any knick-knacks. If you have bad furniture (and can admit it), cover it up with neutral-coloured blankets. Bright orange rugs should probably go into storage and that Canada flag you have covering the second bedroom window should be put away until Canada Day comes around again. Try to make your home feel clean and cozy. Think of it as a blank slate for potential buyers to consider their options.

Touch

Like it or not, when you show your home, strangers will be touching your stuff. They will run their hands along the banister, sit on your couch, maybe even on your bedspread. They may use your bathroom. You want to be sure that every surface they come into contact with is clean and smooth. If it's wood that needs resurfacing or brass that needs polishing, do it before potential buyers arrive to size up the value of your space.

Smell

This goes back to my wet-dog example from earlier in this chapter. You want your house to smell inviting. It's for this reason you so often hear the advice that you should bake bread shortly before showing your home. If you aren't much of a cook, you may want to simply try putting fresh-cut flowers in one or more of the rooms. Save the fish dinners for the restaurant during the time your house is up for sale, since fish smells can linger and be a turnoff to your guests.

Air fresheners help. If you have pets, make sure they haven't left any surprises in certain rooms you rarely use. Even the most well-behaved dog or cat can be thrown by the smell of strangers in the house, and leave behind their own gifts in protest. My dog did this once, about half an hour before a showing of my Toronto loft. I did the best I could to clean the mess, but wasn't surprised that those buyers didn't call my agent to ask more questions about my space.

It's Not Just What's Inside that Counts

When you're selling a house, you also have to consider how it looks from the outside.

In 2005, the Royal LePage House Staging Poll found that the exterior of your house is just as important as the interior. Homebuyers look at the exterior first, then decide whether or not to look inside a house. When asked what they thought was the most important exterior feature, the number one answer among prospective buyers was a well-maintained yard (40 percent). A clutter-free yard and driveway ranked second (28 percent), while a newly painted exterior was third (18 percent).

If you're selling, you need to consider what's known as "curb appeal." To get good curb appeal among buyers, you should consider a number of things.

- Keep the yard mowed, raked, weeded, fertilized and watered.
- Trees and shrubs need to be pruned and trimmed.
- Put away hoses, tools, lawnmowers and other outdoor clutter.
- Keep outdoor furniture clean.
- Paint or stain doors, deck and window trim if necessary.
- Sweep the deck, walkway and front sidewalk.
- Create outside living area with furniture and plants.

Curb appeal is very important when selling your home, and making the place nice indoors and outdoors will help you attract the best price possible. Condo owners have little control over the exterior of their buildings, but here's hoping those maintenance fees you've been paying are being put to good use.

Showtime!

You have scrubbed, repaired and organized your home. Now it's time to show it off to potential buyers. Here are a few tips from our friends at

Canada Mortgage and Housing Corporation on staging your home on the day of an open house—or any day that the house will be shown.

- Open all drapes, blinds, etc. and turn on lights to make the house bright.
- Air out the house to get rid of cooking, pet odours, etc.
- Have fresh flowers in view.
- Pick up clutter, and empty garbage.
- Make sure everything is spotless.
- Set your thermostat at a comfortable level.
- Remove pets from the house or put them outside.
- If you have an agent, leave when the house is being shown. If you are selling it yourself, you need to strike a balance between being helpful and crowding the buyer.
- In poor weather, provide a place for boots, overshoes and umbrellas.
- If selling in winter months, display photos of the house and yard in summer to show landscaping.
- Leave out heating and hydro bills for inspection.
- For those on a septic system and/or well, leave out inspection and maintenance information.

The Offer

Remember when you put in the offer for that house? Remember how you strategized to get the lowest price possible, and how you negotiated for extras, a specific closing date and the seller's first-born? Well, now the shoe is on the other foot. You are the "vendor" and your job, along with your agent, if you have one, is to get yourself the best price possible.

The offer process is the same as you read about in Chapter Five, but now you are on the receiving end. The potential buyer will present you with an offer, and you will either accept or reject it.

Rejecting it could mean the bidder walks away, or it could start the ball rolling for some back-and-forth negotiation. Either way, be prepared. Above all, try not to get emotional. Remember Esther's advice from earlier? Sellers often think their home is worth more than it really is, because it's their precious space.

You may get lucky, which many sellers have in the recent hot real estate market, and get a bidding war going. Remember, though, many bidding wars are a result of sellers asking for a price below market value—to create a bidding war. It's a strategy you may want to try, or avoid, depending on the market at the time you sell, because it can backfire: your lowball asking price could send the wrong message to prospective buyers about the home's true value.

The Negotiation

If you've hired an agent, this is where they earn that commission you're paying. Having done this three times in the past, I prefer to have my bulldog agent talk to the potential buyer (and their bulldog agent) and argue it out. This doesn't mean letting your agent decide what price you should sell your home for, though. At the end of the day, it's your call. But keep in mind that a good agent has a lot more experience than you do when it comes to your real estate market.

If you are selling on your own, you have to act as though you were a professional agent. This means leaving the emotion locked in the bathroom and remembering it's a business deal, even if the negotiations end up involving the antique dining room set your grandmother gave you.

Here are some tips for negotiating the sale of your home:

- Keep it professional. This means biting your tongue when the potential buyer tries to use your shag carpet and the flowered wallpaper as an excuse to lower the price. (After all, I told you to tone it down!)

- Tell the truth. If the buyer sees stains on the ceiling from a roof leak, tell them when the flood was, and whether or not you've fixed the problem. Lying is a bad way to begin negotiations.
- Don't get emotional. Don't agree to a dramatic price drop for the couple who recently went down to one income but talk about how in love they are with your space. Remember, it's a business deal. Also remember the advice you got when you bought the home: never fall in love with your property!
- Be flexible. While I was a bit of a curmudgeon in regard to this point, you should be prepared to lower the price a little bit in a negotiation. This also means possibly dropping the price if the home inspection turns up any problems. The exception of course is with a bidding war, when your job is to choose the best bid. This isn't always the highest bid, but rather the bid with an attractive price, and the fewest conditions.
- Explain. You or your agent may need to tell the potential buyer how you arrived at your asking price. This means highlighting positive attributes of your home and why it is so special. Remember, you are selling the features of this place you called home.
- Be objective. The cost of holding out for your best price could actually cost you more in the long run. If you are paying $1,500 a month to keep the property, selling it for $2,000 below asking may be smarter than losing this deal and not having another come along for months.
- Find out more about the buyer. If you have an agent, he or she will do this digging; otherwise, it's up to you. Just as you were told to get pre-approved before making an offer, you'll likely want the same from your potential buyer. If they haven't been pre-approved, chances are it will be a condition of the offer.

- Make the closing date work for you too. The buyer will propose a closing date, but be sure it suits you as well as them. The closing date should give you enough time to move into your next home.

Bring Back Your Lawyer

Remember that little old man (or feisty young woman) who helped you buy your house way back when? You signed some papers, talked about land transfer tax, title insurance; you nodded your head even though you may not have fully understood what they were saying (maybe because you didn't have this book back then)? Well, call him or her up again. You need a lawyer to help you close the transaction.

Luckily, selling your home costs less in lawyer fees than when you bought. If you are selling your house on your own, you will want to contact a lawyer long before an offer is made. He or she will give you some advice on what needs to be in that contract. It's also probably a good idea if you are selling alone to go back and look at the offer you made when you were a buyer.

If you are selling a condo, you will have to get the status certificate information in order as well. Often the condo corporation will do this for you, but it's still your responsibility to ensure the information gets to the buyer in the timeframe set out in the contract (usually 10 days).

The Winner Is...

You've found a buyer, signed the offer and all conditions have been met. Congratulations, you've sold your home!

There are a few things to remember before you hand over the keys on closing day. First, there's probably a clause in your sale agreement that allows for the buyer to perform a walk-through of the property just prior to closing. They will be checking to ensure any required repairs have been done, and that the home is in the same condition as when they made the offer. You, the seller, are responsible for any problems that arise before the deal officially closes.

On closing day, your lawyer will handle all the paperwork, including ensuring all taxes, loans and liens are paid. The lawyer will also transfer the deed and ensure the funds from the buyer are transferred to you. Once this is complete, you have officially moved on.

Beth, the online editor you know from previous chapters, calls the sale of her first home in St. John's "fairly painless." She got some good advice from her agent on how to present her home to potential buyers, but the selling time took longer than she had expected.

She says selling the house was made easier by seeing how much the buyer loved the property. "I thought I would be more emotional about the house, but I didn't have any of those pangs," Beth says. Since she sold the home, Beth has been invited back—as a guest.

Just as Beth was able to do, it's best if you can avoid getting too emotional about a house you're leaving behind. Every home you've ever been in has its good memories, and its bad ones. Remember there was a reason you sold this one, and you should look forward to your next home, wherever that may be.

Checklist: When It's Time to Sell

✓Find an agent, or decide you will act on your own to sell the home.

✓Determine the market value of your home and set your price accordingly.

✓Fix repairs needed on your home to help present the best product to potential buyers.

✓Clean out clutter such as excess furniture, memorabilia and knick-knacks. Your goal is to present a clean, open, comfortable home.

✓For showings, let as much light in as possible. Open windows, turn on lamps, light candles and play soft music to present an attractive space. Remove any odours from everyday living, such as cooking and pet odours.

✓Be professional when dealing with offers from potential buyers.

✓Be reasonable when it comes to offers that are lower than asking; you may have to budge on price if you really want to sell your home.

✓Hire a lawyer to help you close the deal. Just like when you bought your home, lawyers will wrap up the financial details and transfer the deed to the new owner.

✓Celebrate. Congratulations, you've sold your home. Now you're ready to move on to your next living adventure.

Common Mistakes to Avoid:

✗ Acting as your own agent. If you aren't ready for the hard work it takes to list, advertise, show and negotiate your own home sale, it's often worth the price of the commission to hire a real estate agent instead.

✗ Not fixing problems before you post the for-sale sign. While many buyers are interested in "as is" products, chances are you won't get the best price. Even the suggestion that a home needs work can drive down the price. Make repairs if possible. This allows you to ask the very best price for your home.

✗ Showing too much personality. Home buyers want to picture themselves living in your space. So get organized, store some furniture and most of all—clean up!

✗ Talking too much. Even if you're desperate to sell, potential buyers shouldn't know it. Remain calm: your house will sell.

✗ Getting too emotional. As we have advised for both buying and selling, falling in love with your property can only break your heart. Don't get attached to real estate.

11

Buying a Second
Property

---

*I*f you just bought your first home as a single woman, or are still saving up for one, talking about buying a second property may sound far-fetched. But while it may sound impossible now, there may come a time when you'll be ready and want to purchase a second property, such as a cottage or chalet. Carrying one home is a lot of responsibility. Carrying two can be twice as difficult, or twice as enjoyable, depending on you, your personality, and of course, your finances.

In this final chapter we'll take a look at second properties and help you decide if you're a monogamist or not when it comes to owning property.

Are You a Two-Home Woman?

Before you sign up with a real estate agent in cottage country, do a little navel-gazing. Are you really the type to carry two properties?

Everyone returns from a weekend in the country or a vacation thinking how great it would be to come back to the same lovely location every weekend. It's probably a good idea to impose your own cooling-off period between the vacation and any decision to buy a second property in that place. Think very carefully about how much time you would actually spend in that second home. Are you the type of person who buys a one-year gym membership and never goes? How about your car lease—have you ever kept a vehicle for the entire three- or four-year term, or did you get bored and trade it in for a new model with a nicer colour? Finally, let's get personal here—what about your relationships? Of course your dating habits and housing aren't linked (are they?), but only you know what kind of a commitment you are able to make. A second property is a commitment, just like your primary residence. Think it through. Is this the one?

Don't forget the carrying costs of a second home. These include all those extras you're already paying for in your primary residence, everything from taxes and insurance to condo fees (if applicable), utilities, landscaping and other services. A second home means a second set of furniture—bed, couch, dining room table—and a second set of dishes, towels, television, DVD player. The list goes on.

Doug Heldman, a Toronto real estate agent, says anyone buying a second property should sit back and consider how much they will use it. "It's all about time. If it's a second property that has a lawn, or it has bushes that need to be attended to, or snow shovelling or general maintenance—it all takes time. You are there to relax; you don't need those household chores."

Doug is reminded of this on Friday nights in the summer when he sits on his sailboat on Lake Ontario, watching cottagers sitting in their cars on the highway struggling to get out of town. And then there's the commute back into the city. "A lot of people end up leaving the cottage at noon on Sunday to beat the traffic," Doug says.

Still, if you are amenable to making the trip and spending time on a second home, Doug suggests you also consider how long a weekend commute you want to take. That should determine where you begin your search for a second home.

Another consideration is when you should buy a second property. In good economic times, people buy recreational properties, which pushes prices up (consider the recreational property boom in recent years). On the flipside, when economic times are bad, "the first thing they are going to sell is the recreational property," Doug says.

Doug says timing is more important for recreational properties than for primary residences, because even in economic downturns, people need a place to live, and tend to hang on to their existing homes. When it comes to buying a second property, Doug advises, "Think about where you are in a real estate cycle. Timing is everything."

This advice isn't meant to be a deterrent, but you do need to stop and assess your lifestyle and whether a weekend retreat is the right choice for you—and your finances.

Kathryn, the fifty-something Toronto market research consultant who bought and sold two investment properties in Toronto, settled on a cabin in Haliburton, Ontario, north of Toronto, as her second home. "I always wanted to have something on a lake, and toyed with the idea of buying a cottage for years. What held me back were two things, equally important. First, I'm not a 'loner,' and was concerned that I would be forced to bring people with me all the time [that is, entertain guests], or be alone. Second, I didn't have the skills or the inclination to be responsible for all the maintenance and upkeep—worrying about septic systems, grounds maintenance, etc. One house is enough for that."

She settled on a cabin that is part of a co-op, a rare opportunity for second-home seekers. The co-op lifestyle means there is a full-time caretaker, and little or no maintenance other than some raking of leaves in the spring. "I open the front door in the spring, put a chair and a small barbecue outside, dust a little and start enjoying myself. When I saw the property and the cabin, and had the set-up explained to me, I took out my chequebook on the spot!"

Financing the Second Home

The first thing to know about financing a second home is that special rules may apply.

If you are borrowing more than 75 percent of the purchase price of the second property, you will probably need insurance through the Canada Mortgage and Housing Corporation. CMHC has requirements and guidelines when it comes to loans for second homes, such as the following.

- The borrower/owner intends to live in that space at some point during the course of a year, or a relative of the owner would live there rent-free.
- The property can be located anywhere in Canada but must be suitable and available for year-round occupancy. Properties constructed for seasonal use, or with only seasonal access, are not eligible.
- Properties located on an island must have year-round bridge or ferry access.
- The property cannot be a time-share interest, life lease or be in a rental pool.

When it comes to qualifying for a second-home mortgage, your income is what counts. Any rental income you might get from the second property doesn't count. If you plan to put down more than 25 percent of the purchase price, the bank won't be as concerned about how you use the property, says Toronto-based mortgage broker Bryan Sutter.

They still may ask questions, however. "Marketability is always a concern for the bank. For example, if a property is only accessible by boat, only those people with boats would be interested in buying it. This is important to the bank in case they have to take over the property and sell it," Bryan explains. If there are no concerns about marketability, he says, and the down payment is substantial, there probably won't be a problem with how you intend to use the property: "You can buy a cottage or rental with 25 percent down, with no intention of occupying the subject property."

It's best to check with your lender to see what the latest requirements are to qualify for a second-home mortgage.

In terms of mortgage rates, there shouldn't be much difference between mortgage rates on a loan for a primary or secondary residence. Rates are typically higher for investment properties because lenders see them as more risky ventures. But Bryan says that "buying a second home for vacation or rental purposes is almost as easy as buying a home to live in." It all comes down to your income. "Keep in mind that you have to be able to afford your current residence in addition to the mortgage and taxes on the second property."

Again, check with your lender on the terms before making an offer on a recreational property.

Before You Go Second-Home Hunting

The process of buying a second home is not unlike the process you went through when buying the first one. You have to do your homework.

Picking where you want to buy your second property is your first task. Because it's your getaway home, your choices are greater than simply being within commuting distance to work. To narrow down your choices, it's best to spend some time in the areas you are considering. This means a weekend, or a week, or more. Living in an area, even on a part-time basis, is a lot different from visiting. If you really want to get a feel for the location, you may wish to rent a place in the area for a few months first.

And because your second home will likely be in an area other than where you live now, it's a good idea to get a new real estate agent. Choose an agent who knows the new area well. Just as I advised in Chapter Two on finding a compatible real estate agent, you should get references and interview a few agents before deciding whom to work with.

The following is a list of tips for finding the perfect second home.

1. **Define your lifestyle interests.** It's well known that people who buy second homes are primarily looking at areas that have to do with their recreational interests. So ask yourself, "What is it that I like to do?"

2. **Determine the ideal travel distance.** Ideal travelling time is a matter of personal preference and tolerance, but it's best to limit yourself to a few hours' travelling time. If it's too far or too expensive to reach within a few hours, you likely won't use an owner-occupied second home enough to justify its cost. Don't sell yourself short by insisting that if you buy it you'll use it. Before you buy, rent in the area for a season. See how often you actually manage to get to your vacation home.

3. **Research locations.** You may like downhill skiing, but can you really afford a home in a ski town? What happens around town when

the slopes close? You've defined your lifestyle, but what about affordability, climate, population and all those other issues? Check with the local chamber of commerce, and use the Internet to find out more about the community you're considering.

4. **Select the desired location and type of home.** Within the destination you have in mind, you'll need to refine your choices. Do you want to be in a new, planned development? Do you want a patio home or townhome for less maintenance? Do you want an inland or a beach community? If you are into beach communities, do you also want a golf community near the beach?

5. **Make inquiries with locals.** Go knock on neighbours' doors to find out what it's like. How many second homeowners are there? Are they true homeowners or renters? Too many renters and they might not be keeping the place up. You need community details often available only from the residents.

6. **Contact a real estate professional in the area.** A real estate professional is your eyes and ears in distance places. You can do a lot of things without a real estate agent, but there is a point when that picture you saw and that virtual tour isn't enough. A realtor can highlight areas of interest. One of the things to remember is that a resort real estate agent is very different from a regular real estate agent in a resort area. You have to rely upon someone who knows the area from a recreational point of view, rather than someone who merely sells homes.

7. **Visit destinations.** Most people will visit a destination two or three times before they purchase. You start finding out about the resources, what the travel time is really like if you drive or fly. Many people who buy a second home are planning, in the back of

their minds, that the property will someday be their primary one. Are you really sure this is where you will want to live?

8. **Review financing options.** Some places deal with high-end purchases that are almost always without loans. Can you use your equity line to buy a second home? Financing for a second home may be different, and there may also be different insurance criteria.

9. **Consider purchasing through a resort specialist.** People selling in a resort area know more about a particular area and typically take it very seriously that business comes from the outside. Outsiders' questions are quite different from those inside the area.

10. **Enjoy the process.** This isn't your primary residence and everything doesn't have to be perfect. Have a little fun with it.

(Sources: www.escapehomes.com, www. realtytimes.com)

Once you've found the perfect second home, you still have a lot of work to do before making a wise decision about whether to buy it. Because you aren't living full-time in your second home, you want to make sure that it's well maintained. The last thing you want is a surprise renovation, such as a leaky roof, to sit days or weeks unattended until you spend time again in the second home.

Royal LePage has compiled a guide to inspecting recreational properties that will come in handy when searching, even before you call in the home inspector for that final, close examination of the property.

Guide to Inspecting Recreational Property

Exterior

- Signs of infestation: Check along the foundation, under eaves, around windows, doors, vents, and chimneys for signs of animals or insects. Watch for small piles of sawdust, unsecured holes, nests, signs of chewing, and animal droppings.

- Roof: Look for loose or missing shingles. A sagging roof will mean a costly replacement.

- Decks and stairs: Check for rotten timber, missing nails, warping, and peeled paint. If the deck is listing or sagging it may not be safe.

- Dock: Look for signs of rot, missing nails, and warping. Are the floats and supports in good shape? Are swimming ladders, tie-ups, and other hardware firmly fixed?

- Trees and utility poles: Check for dead or leaning trees or unsecured utility poles that could be a hazard to you or the building.

- Windows and doors: Check the caulking and weather stripping around doors and windows. Check for rot on frames and sills.

- Siding: Examine the siding for loose or missing planks. Look for peeling or bubbling paint.

- Driveway and access roads: Is the driveway full of potholes, puddles, or trenches? Is the access road privately or publicly owned? Find out who is responsible for maintenance and if there are any special conditions concerning its use.

- Septic and water supply: Are the water pump, well, and pipes in good condition? Is there a sewage system or a septic tank or field? How old is the septic system?

Interior

- General state of repair: Is it clean and well kept? Walls in need of paint, loose banisters, stains, and a general state of disrepair may indicate there are other, larger problems the owner has neglected to fix.

continued

- Electrical: Check the fuse box for signs of water damage. Test light switches and outlets. Make sure appliances included in the sale are in good working order.

- Furnace: Check the condition. Turn on the heat and see how well it works (and how noisy it is).

- Water damage: Examine ceilings and walls for stains and bulges. Excessive mildew can be a sign of leaks or poor ventilation.

- Plumbing: Turn on all faucets to test water pressure and hot water. Flush toilets to ensure proper drainage. Examine the base of faucets, bathtubs, and under sinks for signs of water damage.

- Water quality: What is the source of the water? Is it reliable and consistent? Can you drink the water? Does it have any unpalatable odours?

- Security: An unoccupied cottage is an inviting target for burglars. Are there good locks on all outside doors and windows? Is there an alarm system?

(Source: Royal LePage Canada)

Becoming a Second-Home Owner

Buying a second home involves many of the same rules as when you bought that first one. Once you've found the place, had it inspected, checked your finances and made the deal (following advice from previous chapters), you have your second set of keys. Congratulations. If you're this far along, you should be proud. Not only are you a successful second-home owner, but you have a peaceful place that's also a good long-term investment.

Checklist: If You're Thinking of Buying Another Home

✓ Decide if you are second-home material.

✓ Be sure you can afford the second mortgage.

✓ Do your homework on the area where you plan to purchase a second home.

✓ Find a local agent who is familiar with the market.

✓ Check with the bank on the financing terms for the second home.

✓ Make the offer, following the same rules you did for your first home.

Common Mistakes to Avoid:

✗ Not being able to commit to the second-home lifestyle (including chores, maintenance, repairs). Consider how you will feel about leaving your first home on weekends: will you miss it (and the social life you have there), but feel pressured to visit the recreational property because of the money you invested in it?

✗ Not researching the area, or spending enough time there before making the purchase.

✗ Not realizing the added expense of owning a second home, from utilities to maintenance to the cost of travelling between your two homes.

Conclusion
Buy Yourself

$\mathcal{W}$hether you've already bought your first home, are still thinking about purchasing on your own, or are ready to do it for the second, third, or more times, I hope the stories and advice in this book help you make the best decision—for you.

I would like to say that each time I bought property, it got easier. It didn't. That said, each time I did it I was smarter for having asked more questions, and talked to more professionals along the way. As a single woman, I wish I'd had a book like this to guide me through the process. While many real estate books offer great advice on buying and selling, this one is geared for you, the single woman doing it on her own.

The stories and advice don't stop here, though. Visit my website, www.brendabouw.com, where I hope women and professionals can exchange stories and advice particular to their individual home-buying (and selling) needs.

Thanks for reading.

Index

Mark your notes here:

Mark your notes here: